Searching for Paradise

Searching for Paradise

A Story of Chiefs, Gangs, Prime Ministers, and the God beyond the Clouds

CHARLES NOMBO LAPA
and JANET DICKSON

Foreword by Neil Smith
Introduction by Peter O'Neill

RESOURCE *Publications* • Eugene, Oregon

SEARCHING FOR PARADISE
A Story of Chiefs, Gangs, Prime Ministers, and the God beyond the Clouds

Copyright © 2024 Charles Nombo Lapa and Janet Dickson. All rights reserved. Except for brief quotations in critical publications or reviews, no part of this book may be reproduced in any manner without prior written permission from the publisher. Write: Permissions, Wipf and Stock Publishers, 199 W. 8th Ave., Suite 3, Eugene, OR 97401.

Resource Publications
An Imprint of Wipf and Stock Publishers
199 W. 8th Ave., Suite 3
Eugene, OR 97401

www.wipfandstock.com

PAPERBACK ISBN: 979-8-3852-0700-8
HARDCOVER ISBN: 979-8-3852-0701-5
EBOOK ISBN: 979-8-3852-0702-2

01/16/24

All Scripture quotations, unless otherwise indicated, are taken from the Holy Bible, New International Version®, NIV®. Copyright ©1973, 1978, 1984, 2011 by Biblica, Inc.™ Used by permission of Zondervan. All rights reserved worldwide. www.zondervan.com The "NIV" and "New International Version" are trademarks registered in the United States Patent and Trademark Office by Biblica, Inc.™

The New King James, Copyright © 1982, Thomas Nelson, Inc. Used by permission.

The NET Bible, Copyright © 1996–2006, Biblical Studies Press, L.L.C. http://net-bible.com. Used by permission.

We wish to acknowledge the many people who have played significant roles in the Wiru valley, Port Moresby, and Papua New Guinea. This is the story of one man's life, but there are thousands of others not named in this book, who are creators of the ongoing story of Papua New Guinea.

We honor you.

Contents

Foreword by Neil Smith — ix
Preface — xiii
Introduction by Peter O'Neill — xv

PART 1 | THE VALLEY

1	The voice on the mountain	3
2	The village	6
3	The mountain of death	9
4	Warrior Mama	15
5	War and a baby	19
6	The peace child	21
7	A brother in the fire	24
8	The Poku, cannibals and a strange roaring	29
9	The songs of the valley	33

PART 2 | WHITE MEN'S TRIBES

10	The smell of possum and Johnson's baby powder	43
11	Half devil and half child	47
12	Nombo goes to school	55
13	Holy water on the spirit house and a flying angel	62
14	A village of peace	65
15	Badly cooked cabbage and a kiap wants a wife	71
16	The chief goes to jail	77
17	Becoming a man	81

PART 3 | OPENING THE EYES OF THE BLIND

18	The rise of the gangs	89
19	A partner for life	94
20	Gangs, sorcery, and men who can't smile	98
21	Even the birds disappeared	103
22	Public floggings?	106
23	Converting the white heathens	110
24	When gang rape happens, where is God?	114
25	What we need is tanim bel	118
26	The shooting	124
27	Confrontation: 500 gangsters meet the Prime Minister	127

PART 4 | HEAL OUR LAND

28	A light in Galilee	133
29	Building a nation	136
30	A Prime Minister with a broken heart	138
31	A Speaker speaks	140
32	Peace on earth	144
33	Kings and priests	149
34	Crossing into the promised land	155

Bibliography — 159

Foreword

CHARLES LAPA—I FIRST HEARD that name when I was sitting in my office, nervously awaiting my upcoming, face-to-face meeting with the Prime Minister of Papua New Guinea.

Until then, my only knowledge of this nation had come via the stories of my Senior Pastor, Russell Evans, and my wife Leonie, both of whom had been born on the mission field of Wewak, where their parents served the Lord faithfully in the 1960s. It was out of nowhere that I became aware of the familiar 'whisper' of the Holy Spirit, arresting my attention and directing it to this nation, rich in natural resources, but more importantly, rich in its people. I knew that God had deposited a seed of faith in me to see a nation transformed, and there was no turning back!

Through a series of truly 'divine' encounters, meetings, and events, all confirming the whisper of God, I found myself awaiting an audience with the Prime Minister and wondering what I would say to him. All I had was the call, and a promise that God would guide my steps.

It was then that one of our Planetshakers staff members casually mentioned that a family from Papua New Guinea was visiting friends in Melbourne and were available if I would like to meet them. Keen for any insight I could get into the nation, I agreed, and before long sat face-to-face with the Lapa family.

My lasting memory of that first meeting with Charles was of a truly humble man, wholly devoted to his beloved nation. He shared his dreams for his people—dreams to see them restored and prosper under the hand of God, and to see the effects of idolatry washed away through the blood of Jesus. I was moved by his passion for those who were desperately needy both in resource and in spirit: especially his affection for the *raskols*, gangs of trouble-making youths, who were temporarily without vision and purpose for their lives. Clearly, he was a man not prepared simply to talk about his nation's growing issues. He was willing to get his hands dirty at great personal sacrifice for a cause so much greater than himself.

It was only later, when I met with the Minister for Higher Education and former Speaker of the House of Parliament, that I realized the extent of this humble man's influence on his nation.

When Charles Lapa's name came up in conversation, it was mentioned with great affection and endearment: "Charles Lapa—my spiritual father who saved me." I listened as this highly distinguished politician told his personal story of redemption. Charles Lapa had been instrumental in rescuing him at the lowest point of his life, and setting his feet on course for national significance, by introducing him to his faith and becoming his personal mentor. I would come to realize that this was the story of many others, who had discovered their God-given purpose through the love, encouragement, prayer, practical support, and instruction of Charles Lapa.

I have heard many stories since of how the preaching and ministry of Charles Lapa has touched the nation of Papua New Guinea—cities and villages alike. Not the least of his many achievements has been introducing his nation to the Word of God and its power to heal and set people free. His humility and devotion to his country and to his God, have opened doors of influence that testify to his unique calling to bridge skilfully the gaps between government and church, and church and community. He is a true statesman in every sense of the word, and is highly respected among the influential and the seemingly insignificant alike.

He carries a quiet but potent authority and always seeks the positive that is so often buried beneath a sea of negativity. In many ways, he is a modern-day Joseph to the nation of Papua New Guinea.

In addition to being a spiritual father to many, Charles is a wonderful father to his own children, whom he has raised to be wonderful citizens of Papua New Guinea. His beautiful family is perhaps his greatest achievement and legacy.

I am so grateful that God caused our paths to cross in such a supernatural way, and feel very privileged to partner with Charles Lapa to see his ultimate dream fulfilled—that Papua New Guinea would truly become a nation under the Lordship of Jesus Christ.

FOREWORD

There is no one more qualified to tell the stories behind the ongoing transformation of this wonderful nation than Charles Lapa himself. I am certain that his eyewitness account will deeply inspire you, as it has inspired me.

Neil Smith
International Director
Planetshakers
Melbourne, Australia

Preface

When we began to write this book in 2013, we wanted to capture one man's story, which also represented the story of his nation.

10 years later, this narrative seems more important than ever. Fewer people in the lands now known as Papua New Guinea remember life before colonization, so it is vital to keep the stories alive. The children of the future need memories such as these, to understand the rich history of their people.

We also wanted the story to be 'prophetic'—to be a declaration of the rich and beautiful future that is possible for the people of Papua New Guinea. We had a dream, of a future in which Papua New Guinea will become confident in its unique identity as a nation. We saw this land as a nation where goodness, peace, love, righteousness, and glory reigns.

The nations of the world are struggling with identity, and the struggles seem to be increasingly bitter and divisive. Nations are at war with each other, and conflicted within.

We believe that the smaller nations, like Papua New Guinea, will lead the way in showing the world how diverse and warring people groups can be reshaped, one person at a time, and become one nation that is whole, and fully alive.

Charles Nombo Lapa and Janet Dickson

Note: The spelling of words and names in the Wiru language may vary from accepted forms. We have chosen to use spellings preferred by the people in the stories. Some names in this book have been changed, particularly the names of former gang members.

Introduction

THE WIRU TRIBE OF Pangia, Southern Highlands Province, where Pastor Charles and I hail from, had first contact with Western civilization in the 1960s. In fact, the first contact was from the missionaries who brought the Good News of Jesus Christ.

We came the hard way from a simple primitive traditional way of living, to the modern western civilization world we know today, and to becoming the people we are today. Pastor Charles Lapa has emerged as one of the first Papua New Guinean evangelists who has greatly impacted thousands of lives with the Gospel, not only through his crusades, Church ministry, rehabilitation center, Bible College, and Wantok Radio Light prayer program, but also through his influence in the public and private sector, political and government sector, and education sector.

Growing up as a child, I remember watching and listening to him preaching. I have always respected him as a man of God, and as a son of Southern Highlands province who is a pioneer of spreading the Good News through PNG and abroad.

This book, *"Searching for Paradise,"* tells the story of a young boy's search for the meaning and purpose of life, that has seen him achieve great things to this day. It is an inspiring story that will capture the imagination and hearts of its readers.

May Pastor Charles Lapa's vision for seeing positive change and transformation in every Papua New Guinean, especially the youth of the nation, be a vision we all aspire towards.

HON. PETER O'NEILL, CMG
Former Prime Minister of Papua New Guinea

PART 1

The valley

1

The voice on the mountain

The story begins at Mount Ialibu—the sacred mountain, the mountain of life. Many tribes lived in the fertile valley below. Each tribe had its own villages, gardens, and hunting grounds. Every tribe also had a share in the hunting grounds on the lower slopes of Mount Ialibu. This mountain that was the source of their life was like a mother surrounded by her children, each one holding on to a part of the mother's skirt.

The upper part of the mountain was different. The misty peak of Mount Ialibu did not belong to any one tribe, because it was a place for revelations. Only the boldest chiefs climbed through the clouds to the higher parts of the mountain, where they sought dreams and visions from the spirit world. The mountain was their gateway into the invisible realms.

Chief Imbinali never approached the mountain lightly. When he climbed its slopes, he settled down to fast and pray for up to forty days and forty nights, waiting to hear from the spirit world. There were times when Imbinali was hidden in the mists for days, experiencing nothing but swirling whiteness and drizzling cold. On other occasions the clouds would clear and he could see the sunlight spreading over the plains and valleys below.

On the mountain Imbinali saw dreams and visions for his tribe, of things past and things to come. Then he would make the slow descent to the village where his people were waiting. Usually, he said little of what he had seen, but his people knew that these spirit encounters gave him knowledge and wisdom for leading the tribe.

The people of the valley had their spirit houses and their witchdoctors, but Imbinali often told his people, "There is another God, a bigger God who is above all these things." They did not know this God so they called him Akolali, "The God beyond the clouds."

One day Chief Imbinali and his friend Koke Itua went to Mount Ialibu to hunt and to check on their pandanus and karuka nut gardens. They also wanted to wait for dreams for their clans and families. When they reached their mountain hut, Imbinali made a fire where they warmed themselves and cooked some food.

For two days the hunting was poor. On the third night while they were sleeping, they heard a call. Imbinali got up and Koke Itua followed him outside. A voice called, "Tiki!"

It was not quite like a man's voice, but not a woman's voice either. The voice called again, "Tiki!"

It was the name of Imbinali's son, who was about three years old. Imbinali stretched out his hands in the darkness. "A-ye? You speak?"

This was the right response to a revelation from the spirit world. Koke Itua also spoke in his Kewapi language. "R-la? You speak?"

Men from both language groups had heard the voice, so it was expected that both should respond.

The voice called a third time, "Tiki-yaaaaaaeeeeeeh!"

Again, Imbinali replied, "A-ye?" and Koke Itua called, "R-laaaaaaa...?"

Koke Itua's call was long, trailing away like an echo to show that he was ready and waiting to hear more. Both men were accustomed to dreams and visions, but a voice was something new. They realized it must be important.

They waited, their faces raised to the sky, but the voice did not speak again.

The men talked for a long time about what it could mean. Imbinali wondered if something had happened to his family, so at daybreak they gathered their belongings and returned to his village. He found his wife, Lendepame, working in their gardens.

"Did you call?"

Lendepame did not know what he was talking about.

"Where is our son? Has anything happened?"

His wife leaned on her digging stick and stared at him. "He is here. All the children are here."

"They are all safe? There is nothing wrong?"

She pointed to the children, playing among the mounds of taro and sweet potatoes. "Everything is well."

Imbinali and Koke Itua told her what had happened. They went to Koke Itua's village and again asked, "Did anyone call?" But no one had called or heard a voice. The two men had no doubt they had heard the voice of Akolali.

They told the clan leaders about the voice. Imbinali explained, "I think this was the voice of the God beyond the clouds. He is beginning to reveal himself to us, and he wants me to set my son apart for him."

Imbinali decided to wait until Tiki was older before telling him about the call. In the meantime, he and the village leaders waited and watched to see what Akolali would do.

What became of Tiki? This book is the true story of what has unfolded in his life. It is a story of chiefs, gangs, prime ministers, and the God beyond the clouds.

When Tiki was born, he was given two names. In the Wiru language of his father, he was called Nombo, meaning "taro leaf." When rain falls on taro leaves it runs off, so this name meant that accusations against Nombo would not stick to him. The name Tiki is from the Kewapi language of his mother. Tiki also means taro leaf, but in a different sense: tik is taro leaves packed together and cooked like a cake with many layers. Tiki was his special name, but usually his family called him Nombo, so that is the name we will use for the rest of his story.

2

The village

THE VALLEY WHERE NOMBO (Tiki) grew up was a place of quiet beauty, with forests, hills and rolling plains of kunai grasslands. Streams and great rivers watered the valley: some roared as they rushed over rocks and waterfalls, others flowed calmly between grassy banks. There were lakes and marshes, filled with reeds and fish. The forests were quiet places, with tall trees and bright yellow flowers that grew as high as a man's shoulder. Tiny orchids clung to the trees, some in muted creams and browns, others glowing like bright purple jewels.

The forests were rich in provision, with wild animals for meat and bamboo and timber for houses. There were strong saplings for bows and spears, and supple bark which could be made into bowstrings, belts, and clothing. In the clearings, rocky outcrops provided flint stones for spearheads and axes, and larger stones were carved into bowls for cooking and ceremonies. Everything the people needed was there in the valley.

Then there were the birds—huge cassowaries that could outrun a child, water birds on the lakes and rivers, and an array of small forest birds whose calls woke the villages every morning. The loveliest of all were the birds of paradise, with their glorious colors and liquid songs. Every afternoon they would come down into the villages and sing and dance in the trees, like evening guests.

Villages were scattered across the valley. Some had thirty or more dwellings which rested lightly on the landscape, standing on stilts, each house beautifully crafted from carved rosewood and intricately woven bamboo. Every village was slightly different, but each had two long rows of houses surrounded by bare golden earth. The main villages had up to three hundred people, but families also had their own "family villages" elsewhere, like small farms with just one or two houses and shelters for their animals.

Between the rows of houses was an open space like a street, where people would gather, and in times of celebration everyone would dance there. Usually the people were almost naked, with bark belts holding woven loincloths at the front and long *tanget* leaves at the back as their only covering. For celebrations, it was different. Then everyone adorned themselves with extravagant costumes of grasses, feathers, furs, and shells. Money was not needed in the valley, as the currency of trade was salt, kina shells as big as small shields and *pero*, a kerosene-like oil that seeped from the rocks on the other side of the mountain.

People did not go hungry here. Everyone lived on the bounty of the forests, with possums, wild pigs and cassowaries for meat and fish from the rivers. There were annual harvest times when the karuka nuts ripened and the red pandanus produced enormous scarlet fruits as long as a man's arm. These were wonderful times, when different clans met together to trade and to share the produce from their own particular lands.

Each village was surrounded by gardens, cleared by the men, and tended with great skill by the women. They grew sweet potatoes, taro, yams, cucumber, greens, and sugarcane as well as corn and bananas. Women spent most of their time in the gardens every day, digging, hoeing, planting, and harvesting, ensuring an abundant supply of food for every person in the village. No vegetables needed to be stored because some crop was always ready for harvest.

Above all there were pigs. In the Highlands pigs were prized above any other possession, and often women would suckle a baby on one breast and a piglet on the other. Pigs were brought up with the family and the young pigs would trot beside the children when they set off to work in the gardens. While the mother and children worked, the pigs foraged in the grasslands and forest. When a piglet was small, it walked with the family like a puppy on a woven bark lead and was kept tethered while they worked. But when it was older and well trained, it roamed free. In the afternoon, the pigs returned home with the family and trotted straight back to their pig houses. There was no need to drive them because the animals knew where to go.

Pigs were a source of meat, and they were also the most significant part of the family's wealth. A man's status and power could be measured by the number of pigs he owned. They were always the main bargaining point in bride-price ceremonies. When a marriage was being arranged, the woman's family would meet with the family of the groom to discuss the worth of the bride, which was measured in pigs, kina shells, food, and other gifts.

Whenever there were celebrations and ceremonies, there was pig-killing. The pigs were lined up in the center of the village and men dug large firepits for the *mumu* (feast). The men were skilled butchers. They slaughtered the pigs and cut them meticulously into pieces—each piece had a name and particular significance. Fires were lit and large stones were placed in the pits to heat up like an oven. The women wrapped large pieces of meat in leaves, together with yams, sweet potatoes, and taro roots, and placed the parcels in the firepits on top of the hot stones. They heaped the earth over again and the food was left to cook slowly for many hours. When it was time for the feast, the men opened the pits, as excited children gathered to watch. By that time the numbers in the village would have grown because people from miles around would see the smoke from the fires. It was a time for many clan groups to gather, to share news, to form alliances and to enjoy a feast.

Fresh banana leaves were placed in the middle of the men's house (*hausman* or *Poku Wiru*) and the chiefs, clan leaders and headmen gathered there. Young men brought the first parcels of food and placed them on the leaves. The children crowded around the door, peering in to see the food. As the chiefs and leaders began to eat, the rest of the food was distributed to the other men, women, and children outside. There was always enough for everyone.

This was Nombo's world. For a small child, it was paradise.

# 3

The mountain of death

Nombo's valley may have been a paradise, but like every Eden, it contained its own particular serpents. The people of the Wiru experienced sicknesses, jealousies, misunderstandings, and disagreements, as well as outbreaks of devastating diseases like leprosy. However, all these issues paled into insignificance beside the greatest cause of death and destruction: tribal wars.

For generation after generation, tribes and clan groups waged ongoing warfare over land and power. Each battle would bring a level of peace for a time, but for the losing tribe, every defeat became the catalyst for the next round of revenge killings. And so, the cycle continued, year after year. Every man in the valley was a warrior, trained in the arts of combat from infancy.

Nombo first learned to fight with mud. All the little boys lined up facing each other and threw tiny fistfuls of mud at their opponents, learning to duck and weave to avoid being hit themselves. This was enormous fun. Like boys everywhere, they learned to wrestle and push their opponents to the ground. Small boys and girls were taught to use sharp stone axes as soon as they could hold them, and Nombo's first weapon was an axe-head which he used to skin an animal or to carve a rough spear. The children carried their tiny weapons with them everywhere, tucking them into their bark belts just like their elders.

When Nombo and his friends were about five years of age, their fathers and uncles began to train them, saying, "You must learn to be strong and run fast."

Part 1 | The valley

The men took them further and further from the village. The boys learned to run, climb trees, and cross rivers, jumping over ditches and chasing through valleys to see who was the fastest. When the boys were exhausted, the men sat down with them and taught them how to take the soft core of tall plants to use as spears. The children used these soft spears to throw at each other, all little warriors in training.

When the boys were about seven or eight years old, they learned *kalawirapoi*—harder fighting, with bows and arrows. The arrows were not sharpened, so when they hit a boy, they would bruise but not pierce him. The boys learned to aim for the head because in battle they wanted the enemy to die. The most important lesson for each child was how to avoid being hit, especially in the head and chest. The boys loved those battles; no one was hurt, at least not seriously, and just like Western children playing dodge-ball, the winner was the child who survived longest without being struck. After all, a warrior is only great if he survives.

As they grew older, the boys progressed to the next stage known as *yomboi nali*, painting their faces and using a smaller version of adult warriors' weapons. When their beards began to grow, they were initiated and expected to join the other warriors in fighting. Their fathers, brothers and uncles taught them how to make bows, carving them out of saplings and making bowstrings out of finely peeled soft bark. They fashioned bamboo into arrow shafts then lashed on finely carved arrowheads. Usually, the men made spear and arrowheads from animal or cassowary bones, but sometimes they used human bones, such as fingers or ankle bones from young men or chiefs of their tribe who had died. The arrowheads were shaped with great skill so that when they hit a target they would break off, leaving part of the barbed arrowhead in the body of the victim. The warriors believed that if the arrowhead was made of human bone, the victim was more likely to die because the bone carried power from the dead warrior.

Nombo was taught all these things by his father. Chief Imbinali Lapa was the chief of his clan group, the Waimapo, and his larger tribe, the Kawirene, and he was also the accepted leader of the surrounding tribes that traded and fought together in a loose alliance. In the Wiru language, *embin* means name and *ali* means man, the two names together signifying a man with authority. *Lapa* means noise. So Chief Imbinali Lapa was a man of authority, with a voice to be heard. He was not a loud man, but when he spoke, people listened.

The tribes in the Wiru valley generally planned their battles, preferring not to carry out surprise attacks on villages where women and children could be harmed. Imbinali was a renowned warrior, but he liked to fight fairly, with minimal killing. He would meet with the chief of the enemy tribe and agree on a time and place, away from the villages. The battlefield was always carefully chosen, usually a place with a river or cliff along one or two sides to mark the boundaries.

Then the men of the tribe cleared the battleground, ready for action. First, they dug a war trench along their own end of the ground. It ran the full width of the battlefield, about 20 meters across, and it was about a meter wide and deep enough to hide a man.

When the battleground was ready, the warriors went back to the village to prepare their weapons: spears with bone or flint arrowheads, axes, bows and arrows. Their spears and bows were long, as tall as themselves. Nombo and the other boys begged to try their fathers' bows, straining with all their might to pull back the enormous bowstrings, but their arms were never strong enough. The men laughed at them and told them to wait till they were bigger, but sometimes while they worked, they showed the boys how to fashion their own small bows. Each warrior whittled the tip of his bow to a sharp point so it could also be used as a spear. They sharpened their axes with flint stones then tucked the axes and arrows into their belts. They carved wooden shields from strong timber, both long shields and shorter fighting shields. The long shields were used by a group of men known as the shield bearers, whose job was to defend.

Next the warriors prepared themselves, decorating their faces and bodies with paints, shells, and feathers. Imbinali's tribe had adopted the cassowary as their totem because it was swift and strong and ran upright like a man. The children searched for bird of paradise, cassowary and mountain eagle feathers and colored leaves for their fathers and brothers, running back to the *Poku Wiru* (Wiru men's house) with their treasures. As the men wove the leaves and feathers into their headbands, they believed that they were taking into themselves some of the unique spiritual power of their land.

All the children in the village were hugely excited when a battle was being planned. They jostled for places outside the men's house to watch the chief and the warriors as they prepared for war. They waited for the special moment when the chiefs and warriors brought out their kina shells. These were stored in the *Poku Wiru*, wrapped in special pouches made of

Part 1 | The Valley

bark. For important occasions such as ceremonies and battles, the men took down the pouches and unwrapped their most valuable shells, wearing them like breastplates on their chests. The shells were a reminder of past victories and were a show of strength when they came face to face with their enemies. The luckiest boys were the ones whose fathers gave them a kina shell to wear. They would puff out their chests, bursting with pride.

Finally, when all other preparations were completed, the chief brought out a gourd filled with *pero*, the pure kerosene-like oil. It was highly valued and had become a sought-after item for trade, so every chief in the region wanted some to be used by his men in times of war. The village was filled with the sharp odor as they smeared the oil all over their skin to make it harder for the enemy to seize their sleek and shining bodies.

Nombo and the younger children were never allowed to follow the warriors to the battlefield, and they envied the older lads who had been initiated and could join in. On the day of the battle, they watched the men leave for the battlefield before dawn. The women, children and older men waited in the village. They seemed calm, but the whole tribe was on the alert, ready to run at a moment's notice. When any problem or battle was happening, all the other allied clans and tribes had to be told so that they too could be ready for anything.

Imbinali's clan had several hiding places ready in the jungle. They prepared small huts in different locations throughout their lands to use when hunting or in times of danger. They preferred sites near a river as the sound of running water covered any noises they made. If the village was in danger, the whole tribe could move out in minutes, slipping almost invisibly into the jungle. They carried little because they could hunt for food and build shelter anywhere.

When the warriors arrived at the battlefield, Imbinali went through the preliminaries of calling to the enemy chief with threats, offering him the opportunity to surrender or flee. Of course, the enemy chief refused and responded with similar threats. No chief would capitulate without a fight. Then the first skirmishes began like a stylised dance, with the chiefs leading from the front. Chief Imbinali stepped forward first, with his spear in one hand and a short fighting shield in the other. Behind him stood spearmen, then archers with arrows at the ready in their taut bows. At the rear a group of warriors waited with long shields. If the spearmen and archers had to drop back, then the shield bearers would move forward. The warriors would retreat behind the defensive wall of the long shields and re-group. As a last resort, they would jump back over their war-trench. If the enemy tried to follow them, archers hiding in the trench would shoot the enemy warriors as they tried to cross the ditch.

Nombo and the other boys would often sit outside the *Poku Wiru* in their village, listening to the stories of past battles. The older men of the valley still remember those battles today, and their faces light up with delight as they tell the stories. They have no memory of fear, just of the excitement and the sense of pleasure in their fighting skills.

Nombo's favorite story was about the time when his father was nearly killed in battle.

On this morning, the battle was fierce. Imbinali was locked in hand-to-hand combat with a skilled warrior, who raised his spear and pinned Imbinali's foot to the ground—a favorite and effective manoeuvre. The chief was unable to move, twisting and turning as the enemy warrior raised his axe to slaughter him. But Imbinali was strong. He seized the enemy and lifted him bodily off the ground, swinging around and throwing the man over his shoulder to the archers behind, who killed the enemy instantly. They pulled the spear out of Imbinali's foot and helped him to get back behind the war-trench while they finished the battle. It became a famous victory.

When the warriors returned to their village, the medicine men tended to the wounded. They cleaned the men's wounds with ginger and healing leaves, then heated bone needles in the fire. The men bit on ropes while the medicine men stitched up their wounds with fiber string. Normally all the warriors survived and their wounds healed, though most men in the valley lived with at least one or two broken spear or arrowheads in their bodies. It was just a normal part of a warrior's life.

Nombo heard the story of his father's victory often, never tiring of it. He and his friends often replayed their people's battles, filled with a sense of pride in their village, their clan, and their tribe. Like their fathers, they were careful not to glorify one man—not even the chief—because glory and pride belonged to the whole tribe.

Imbinali never spoke of himself as a chief, preferring to live quietly among his people. He worked from dawn till dark every day, lived simply and believed that he should be on equal terms with everyone.

One day Nombo spoke to his father. "Why do you work so hard? Why don't you just stay in the village and take your place as a chief and tell everyone what to do?"

Part 1 | The valley

Imbinali replied, "I am protecting your future."

Nombo did not understand what his father meant. Imbinali did not want to sit in the village talking while others worked. He was trying to accustom his tribe to a different kind of leadership—a leader who serves among his people rather than being a big man. He wanted to raise his sons to lead like this, and he believed it would be better for himself, his children, and his tribe.

Nombo and the other boys expected this life to be their future. They were trained to work the gardens, to hunt, to take a bride and to be a warrior. They did not know that in faraway places a series of events had already begun that would change their lives in the valley forever.

4

Warrior Mama

Chief Imbinali grew in his reputation as a man of wisdom. The people of the Wiru valley said that the sign of a great leader was peace in the land. The best chief was not necessarily the man who was the greatest warrior; he was the man who could maintain peace and stability for his people. Imbinali developed strong relationships with other chiefs and headmen and they formed eight councils throughout the south Wiru, establishing trade and food-sharing alliances, and agreeing to stand together as "fighting friends" in times of war.

Although Imbinali was highly respected in the valley, he was also a source of some puzzlement. Unlike other chiefs, he had only one wife. This was unheard of: many chiefs had five wives who bore them dozens of children. But for some reason, Chief Imbinali always felt that his one wife was enough. And Lendepame was quite a woman.

She came from a village called Tindua, where well-tended houses sat high on a grassy hillside. Her tribe were called the Evari and her father, Irapo, was the chief. Chief Irapo was pleased when his daughter married into a larger tribe because it brought his people security through protection in war, food trade and bride alliances.

Imbinali's people were renowned as warriors and his village was a fighting base, full of vigor and action. Irapo's people were famous for their gardens, and his village had a reputation for being a place of strong women. His clan was seen as being more peace-loving, valuing the skills of women in tending the crops and nurturing children. But Chief Irapo himself, like his father before him, was a fearsome warrior with a reputation for being quick to kill. Even his own family were afraid of his fierce temper.

Like all the villages in the valley, Tindua had separate men's and women's houses. Women were not allowed to come near the men's house, so Lendepame grew up in the women's house with her mother, sisters, aunts, and cousins. The house was solidly built with woven bamboo walls covering a rosewood frame. The roof was thatched with kunai grass. Inside, there was a timber ceiling and a bamboo floor with a large square firepit in the middle. Lendepame and her family were always warm and dry.

Two raised wooden sleeping platforms were set into recesses, one on either side of the room. The women and children all slept together, keeping each other warm through the cold mountain nights. Children were never lonely because there were always others close, both day and night. When Lendepame's brothers were young, they slept in the women's house, but when they began to grow beards, they moved to the men's house for their initiation and training.

A small fire was usually burning in the women's house, with sweet potato, taro or yams baking in the ashes. The family used large leaves for plates and pigs' tusks or gourds for cups. They made mats and clothing from woven bamboo, bark and pandanus fiber.

The first few years after Lendepame married Imbinali was a time of relative peace in their clan. Lendepame brought a different kind of strength to the warrior village, and she worked hard to improve their gardens, spending many hours every day digging, planting, and harvesting the crops. She was skilled in raising pigs and her family prospered. The women were experts at making *bilums* (woven string fabric). They peeled long strips of fiber from various plants and then twisted the fibers tightly together. Once the string was dry, the women wove it into cloth, using only their fingers. Even while they were walking, the women's fingers were constantly moving, twisting, and knotting the bilums into loincloths for their men. The women wore skirts made of *yei*, specially cultivated swamp grasses which they cut and dried over the fire. They wove waistbands then tucked the grasses in, long at the back and shorter at the front.

They wove string bags, also called bilums, which they used to carry everything from babies to firewood. When a mother walked to the gardens, she carried her sleeping baby in a bilum lined with pandanus matting, and she hung the bilum on a tree like a hammock while she worked. At the end of the day, the mother walked home with a heavy load. On her back she carried the sweet potatoes, the green leafy vegetables, and the baby. She packed firewood in another bilum and carried this in front. Lendepame was fit and strong, accustomed to walking for miles with heavy loads.

Even though the men were the trained fighters, the women were not weak or timid creatures. They were skilled with an axe or a club and at times women also became warriors. Usually, parents arranged marriages for their children, but the young people often had their own ideas, and occasionally two girls would take a fancy to the same young man. When this happened, the women had a unique way of resolving the situation: each of the two girls chose several women to support her and they fought it out.

When Nombo was still small, his mother was asked to support her younger sister in one of these battles. The whole village gathered in anticipation as the women armed themselves with long poles as big as small tree trunks. The excitement was intense. The two groups of women lined up in the middle of the village to face each other. A command was given and the lines ran towards each other. They swung their huge poles at their opponents, sometimes using them as clubs, sometimes holding them across their bodies to protect themselves. Supporters from both sides cheered their friends on.

It was brutal but no one died, because their aim was to knock their opponents unconscious, not to kill them. Lendepame was ferocious, knocking one woman after another to the ground and leaving one of her opponents unconscious in the thick of the battle. By the time the fight was over, about twenty women were lying dazed and injured, but Lendepame and a few of her comrades were still standing. Their opponents admitted defeat and the victor claimed her man. The bruised and battered women recovered and no one seemed to hold grudges.

But what about the young man? Did he have any say in the matter? The old people today chuckle and say, "He always married the girl. When he had seen the way she could fight, he would not dare to say no."

Although the village was a place where both men and women were accomplished fighters, there was one kind of violence that Chief Imbinali would not allow, and that was men's violence against women. He often said to the men of his tribe, "Your wife carries your name. If you beat her, she carries your mark. Is this what you want others to see?"

He told the men of his tribe to keep their fighting skills and their strength for wars against enemies and not to harm their wives. This was in stark contrast to the reality in many other tribes, where men routinely hit or beat their wives. In Ialibu today, a school teacher remembers how his grandfather had nine wives and shot several with his bow and arrow, because "the food wasn't ready" or because "they treated him with disrespect."

Imbinali broke the pattern in his clan. Over time, the south Wiru valley became a place where many men took just one wife and where violence against women decreased. Despite Imbinali's decision to abandon polygamy, his clan grew rapidly. They joined with the Ai and Kaipa clans and increased to over a thousand people. Eventually Imbinali was accepted as the overall leader of the entire Kawirene tribe.

5

War and a baby

DESPITE PERIODS OF PEACE, it was never long before wars broke out again. Disputes over land, grievances from past killings, personal jealousies and envy over perceived wealth or power—all these things simmered constantly. From time to time the simmering boiled over into open warfare.

When Nombo was barely more than a baby, a series of wars began that was worse than anything the tribe could remember. Chief Imbinali's people engaged in one battle after another against a tribe led by Chief Yapera. Imbinali's home village, Kalane, was situated high on a hillside overlooking the south Wiru valley, and his lands extended from Tindua in the north-west all the way down to the Yalo River[1] in the south. Yapera's home village was Poloko, just a few kilometers north of Kalane, and his tribal lands stretched from Poloko to the hills and forests beyond the Polu River.

Their main battlefield was near Poloko. Battle after battle was fought there for several years. Many men died, but neither side could secure lasting victory. Eventually, at one particularly intense battle, Yapera's tribe inflicted a crushing defeat on Imbinali's warriors, chasing them all the way back to their home villages. All the men, women, and children of Kalane had to run for their lives into the jungle.

For Lendepame this was a terrible moment. She had just given birth to a new baby boy that morning. She already had a young daughter called Takuame and a son called Neri, as well as Nombo, who was three years old. Lendepame knew she could not carry her new baby as well as Nombo,

---

1. The more common spelling is Yaro. We have chosen to use the spelling that the local people said they prefer for Wiru words and place names.

who was too small to run. Lendepame made the most difficult decision of her life: she held her baby close for one last time, then laid him down. She picked up Nombo, told Takuame to hold Neri's hand, and ran with tears flowing down her cheeks, leaving her baby behind. She never saw him again.

They disappeared into the forest. They ran for a long time, and eventually the sounds of the enemy faded. Lendepame's family were safe. Nombo and the other children of the tribe grew up with the story about the tiny baby who was sacrificed so they could live. Lendepame told Nombo that the little baby looked just like him. She never quite recovered from her decision to abandon her son and carried that sadness for the rest of her life.

Their villages were destroyed and the tribe was scattered. Most families sought refuge with other relatives. Imbinali's family went to Lendepame's village to ask for help from his friend Koke Itua, who gladly offered them a home. They stayed there for several years.

Imbinali's tribe was in disarray, but over about five years he gradually regrouped his warriors and they regained strength. They gathered allies who had also suffered at the hands of Yapera's tribe, and together they prepared weapons and planned a new assault. They won a series of small battles, each time killing more of Yapera's men, weakening his tribe, and loosening his hold on the valley. They reclaimed some of their lands and began to rebuild their villages.

Imbinali was glad for the victories, but his heart was not focused on war and revenge. He was looking for a new way to build peace.

6

The peace child

CHIEF IMBINALI PLANNED TO secure peace in the valley through a peace child. This tradition was practiced in many parts of the Highlands: sometimes a chief would give his baby son to a neighboring tribe, or two warring chiefs would exchange children as a promise of future kinship in place of enmity.

Chief Imbinali proposed giving his daughter, Takuame, in marriage to Yapera's brother. If they married, the blood lines of the two tribes would be mingled and there would be less incentive for either side to go to war again since war would mean killing their own kin. In addition, Imbinali's tribe had killed many of the sons of Yapera's tribe, so his daughter would become part of the compensation: she would bear sons to make restitution for the young men who had been lost.

Imbinali's clan leaders agreed and approached Yapera, who consulted with his clan leaders. They, too, were tired of the killing and grieving over the loss of so many of their men, so they agreed that Takuame should be given to Kepe, Yapera's younger brother. Because Takuame was to be a peace child, Imbinali's tribe did not ask for the usual bride price. However, Yapera's clan had their pride and offered a bride price anyway, so negotiations began.

But one person was not happy—Takuame herself! She had grown into a spirited young woman with strong opinions. She already had her eye on a handsome young man in her own tribe and told her parents that she preferred him to a stranger from an enemy village. At first, she flatly refused to cooperate, saying she would not go. Imbinali and Lendepame had a difficult time persuading her that the decision was not just about her own personal preferences. Finally, her father simply told her, "No, the choice is not yours. You are looking at a handsome face, but we are looking at the future of our tribe. We have made the decision: you will be a peace child."

In the end she agreed. After all, it was the way of the valley that young men and girls were guided by their elders in the choice of a husband or wife. Takuame did not lack courage and understood that the survival of her people was at stake. Imbinali and Lendepame began the arrangements for her marriage.

For the boys Neri and Nombo, the most exciting part of Takuame's marriage was the bride-price ceremony. Takuame and her family all dressed up as devils in full war dress, showing they were ready to fight, then they went to Kepe's village to fetch the bride price. Yapera's tribe also prepared in war dress for the occasion. Dozens of squealing pigs were tethered to stakes in a long line through the middle of their village. Piles of salt, stone axes and gleaming kina shells were hung on poles in front of Yapera's house, together with woven mats and baskets, belts, bilums and gifts of food.

Takuame's bride-price was distributed among the clans. When a family or chief received wealth, it was meant to be shared; no chief in the Wiru valley hoarded goods for himself. In this way, every family and clan group in the valley shared in times of prosperity, valuing the common good and community above individual acquisitiveness. Imbinali distributed the goods among his extended family and allies, honoring his friends and strengthening their relationships. Many people from his tribe came to Yapera's village to receive their share and carry it home.

The ceremonies were completed and Takuame became the peace child, given to seal ongoing peace between two warring tribes. She moved to Yapera's village, Poloko.

For the first few months, Takuame came home once or twice a week, bringing some of her new relatives with her. She brought birds or possums back to her family, and in return her parents gave her meat or foods to eat while she was developing her own garden. Sometimes Nombo went to stay with his sister and the sons of the enemy tribe became his friends.

The peace child arrangement worked: there have been no wars between these two tribes since Takuame was given in marriage. She became a happy and capable mother and bore five healthy sons who each have sons of their own, so the honor of the tribe was restored. The two chiefs, Imbinali and Yapera, became the best of friends, and Yapera trained Takuame's oldest son to share the leadership with him. Forty years later, their tribe continues to live in peace, and Takuame is still a woman of spirit.

As peace in the valley became more established and an increasing number of tribes joined their alliance, eventually Imbinali found himself recognized as the overall chief of several thousand people.

Although his father had been renowned as a leader in the valley, Imbinali did not automatically inherit the same right to lead; he had to earn respect for himself in two important ways. First, he had to demonstrate he could provide for his family group and his tribe, particularly that he had enough pigs to maintain the all-important cycles of pig-killing. Then he had to demonstrate he was a peacemaker who could win and secure stability in their lands.

Imbinali had now proven himself on all counts. He and Lendepame had prospered, owning more than thirty pigs, and managing extensive lands. He had gained a reputation as a wise and generous leader within his tribe, and he was a fearless warrior, capable of leading his men to victory. Most importantly, he had proved that he was skilled not only in making war but also in making peace.

The people of the south Wiru began to prosper, sharing together in the abundance of the valley.

7

A brother in the fire

Nombo's young life had already been eventful, with tribal wars and then his sister's marriage. But he was still a small boy, cheerfully unaware of the seriousness of events in his tribe. He knew only that he was with his family and that he had enough to eat.

For Nombo, the highlight of Takuame's bride price ceremony was a group of baby cassowaries, scrambling over each other and chirping in fright. Most of the young birds were given away to Nombo's uncles, but his family kept one baby cassowary or *kembi*.

Nombo helped his father build a small house for the bird so that it would not run back into the jungle. The young *kembi* became the family's pet. Every morning Nombo ran to the enclosure and let it out for its morning exercise. The little bird followed the children into the jungle to run and play, chasing them wherever they went.

Every afternoon the cassowary followed the children home where they fed it. This had to be done before nightfall because they believed that a cassowary must never see the fireflies which appeared after dark. None of the children knew why—it was just one of the many stories they were told about how to live. Their parents and uncles taught them that if a firefly came into a house, it signaled danger or poison, and there would be a death in the family. Nombo did not question this. He just avoided fireflies, and every day he brought his pet back to its house and fed it before nightfall so it could close its eyes in sleep before the first fireflies appeared.

As the cassowary grew older, it ran faster, stretching out its long neck and wings and singing loudly. There were times, especially in the late morning and early afternoon, when the *kembi* seemed to go wild, chasing the children with outstretched wings, and pushing them to the ground. When the bird was young this was a wonderful game, but as it grew into a fully-fledged *kurupi*, the children could not play with it any more. A full-grown cassowary's claws are long and sharp enough to kill a pig, so even the men were wary of them. The large bird was kept now in a strong timber enclosure until it was ready to be killed. When a cassowary was killed, everyone was given a small share of the meat. If any clan did not get their share, they would leave the alliance.

The forest was the children's playground. Even the smallest child knew every inch of the surrounding jungle and could recognize precisely the sounds of birds and the scent of animals. Nombo was not afraid of the forest and he and his friends played there for hours, exploring their lands and hunting for birds and animals with their small spears and bows.

By this time a younger brother, Wama, had been born, and he and Nombo became the best of friends. When Wama was old enough, they would climb on the rope vines in the jungle, scrambling high until they could see for miles over the trees and hills. They loved running down to the rivers to swing on the ropes and dive into the lagoons. The two brothers were like monkeys, chasing each other and jumping from tree to tree in their father's garden lands.

Later Imbinali would see his precious trees bent and broken and call his sons. "Who has done this? We need those trees to grow straight for firewood and poles. Who has been climbing them?"

Each boy pointed to the other. "It was him!"

Imbinali taught Nombo how to hunt and trap birds and animals. Large birds which were good to eat came down to the trees near the gardens at night. Imbinali showed his son how to look for bird droppings during the day so that they knew exactly where the birds slept. They prepared a track carefully, breaking off twigs and clearing away dead leaves so they could walk there silently. Then when the moon was full, Imbinali told Nombo it was time to go hunting.

The little boy was bursting with excitement as he and his father prepared their bows and arrows. They set out into the night, Imbinali leading the way. Nombo was terrified of demons or strange things coming up behind him, but he said nothing to his father because he was trying hard to be brave. They found the bird droppings, then both took their bows and shot into the trees. Nombo's fear was forgotten as he and his father picked up the dead birds and carried them home.

He learned how to trap possums. Imbinali watched where possums went in the forest so he knew which paths they used and where they fed. He showed Nombo how to prepare a young tree, bending it over to make a kind of bridge for the possums. He did not put a trap there immediately because the possums would smell the human scent and avoid it. After a month the smell faded and new shoots began to come out of the young trees, then the first possum would cross the bridge and others would follow.

When the possums were accustomed to the route it was time to set a trap with a spring and a rope. Imbinali taught Nombo where to place the traps, setting only one trap in each part of their hunting grounds so they did not kill too many possums by over-hunting. Every morning, Imbinali checked the traps and collected the possums.

Most days, Nombo worked in the gardens with his mother and other families from the village. Every morning they got up and had something to eat. Then Lendepame and the older children gathered their bilums, their stone axes, flint knives and digging sticks. Large bones made excellent digging tools—usually the long bones from the leg of a cassowary. The children untied the pigs in the pig house and led them outside. One of the older children fetched smoldering wood from their firepit to carry with them, and they set off—a cheerful group of women, men, children, and pigs striding through the morning mists and rain, ready for a day's work tending to their crops.

The gardens were beautiful places, with luxuriant mounds of *mondo* (sweet potato) growing in large circular beds and *pingi* (green vegetables) and *teye* (herbs) growing around the borders. Yams and taro plants displayed their deep green foliage against the rich brown earth, and there were beds of corn, sugarcane, cucumbers, cassava and tall, red, spiked pandanus plants. They grew banana palms near the trees, where the cultivated land merged into the forests. In the Wiru valley the people were skilled gardeners. They worked one area for five years, then in the sixth year they left that area fallow and moved their crops elsewhere. They called this "healing the land." This cycle of farming allowed the land to regenerate, so the valley remained rich and fertile.

The gardens were a wonderful place for small children. While the people were working, the pigs wandered off to forage for worms and grubs. Even this was carefully managed so that the pigs were released into different areas throughout the seasons. This meant they did not eat too many of the worms and the soil remained healthy. Nombo and the other children hammered strong branches into the ground then tethered the piglets so they could forage at the edge of the forests. Then Nombo and Wama helped their mother in the gardens, digging the rich dark earth, planting the crops, clearing the weeds, and harvesting ripe vegetables for their food. Soon they got tired and Lendepame told them to run away and play.

As well as their houses in the village, every family had a hut in their gardens where they could cook food and shelter from the rain. This was one of Nombo's favorite places to play, especially on wet grey mornings. The garden house was made of wooden posts, with woven bamboo walls and a roof made of thatched grasses. Banana or kunai leaves lined the floor and there was a firepit in the middle. They would light a fire there, using the embers they had brought from their village. They scraped sweet potatoes or yams clean then placed them around the fire to cook. The hut had no door, so they hung banana leaves over the doorway to keep out the rain and insects.

One day Nombo and Wama were playing in the garden hut together. Nombo was about five years old and his brother was about three. They discovered a new game: one of the boys would take a stick from the fire and set fire to the banana leaves hanging in the doorway. When the flame caught, the brothers would quickly beat it out, then the other one would start again. It was a cold rainy morning, and the two little boys were having the time of their lives.

Then Nombo had to go outside to relieve himself among the trees. He was only away for a minute or two, but when he turned to come back, he stared in shock: the hut was on fire. There was smoke everywhere and the whole doorway was a wall of flames. He began to run, shouting his brother's name and hoping desperately that Wama was already outside somewhere. But he could not see him.

Then he heard Wama's terrified scream from inside the hut: "I'm in here!"

Nombo had no time to think. He knew that if he did not act immediately, Wama would die. He ran through the burning leaves in the doorway, dropped low under the smoke and shouted again, "Where are you? I can't see you!"

Again, Wama called, "I'm here!" He was crouched down, curled up into a tight ball in the back corner of the hut. By this time the bamboo walls and grass roof were blazing.

Nombo crawled to his brother, grabbed him, and dragged him out of the hut.

Neither of the boys was hurt. They stood shivering together in the rain as they watched their family's hut burn to the ground, wondering what their parents would say. However, when their parents saw what had happened and heard their story, they were just delighted that both boys were safe.

Nombo says today that he should have known better than to encourage Wama to play that game. Wama calls Nombo a hero. He says his big brother ran into the flames to save him, and that is what he has done all his life: if Nombo sees someone in trouble, he is willing to risk his own life to rescue them.

8

The Poku, cannibals and a strange roaring

LIFE AND DEATH WERE never far apart in the Highlands. Each tribal and clan chief had his own *Poku* (men's house) in the heart of the village. It was a place of authority, like a village parliament, where the business of the tribe was discussed, events were interpreted and decisions were made. Women and children were not allowed within the walls—only initiated men.

The *Poku* was a place where life and death issues were discussed. If a man had committed wrongdoing, such as killing or poisoning, he was expected to come to the *Poku* to tell the other men. It was not the custom to speak directly—he must speak in a parable saying, "I jumped into the water with all my clothes on."

Others understood he had done something wrong, and all the men would discuss what to do about it.

Sometimes a man would start walking up and down in the middle of the village, shouting angrily, and everyone would know that meant there was trouble in the clan. The talk would begin, accusations like theft or sorcery would be made and fights would break out. The discussions in the *Poku* were not always peaceful. Imbinali hated the endless words and arguments, and although he was a chief, he wanted nothing to do with these village problems.

When a chief died, usually the leadership passed to his firstborn son, but there were times when this did not work. If the oldest son did not want the role, or if he didn't meet the expectations of his people, then sometimes another clan member would emerge and step up to lead. The firstborn son might remain the clan leader, but his kinsman would "speak for him."

Imbinali's father had been the most powerful chief in the south Wiru valley. He was a forceful man, with many wives. A man in his clan dreamed that the chief should not climb a karuka nut tree because it would mean danger for him, but the chief did not listen to the warning and climbed a nut tree. The branch broke and he fell to his death. This was a tragedy for the tribe because the death of the chief was like a victory for the enemy tribes.

When the chief died, his eldest son, Imbinali, was just a small child and too young to assume leadership. So, his uncle, Tunoli, the chief's brother, became the tribe's leader. Tunoli saw himself as a caretaker until Imbinali grew up. But when Imbinali was old enough to take over the leadership, he did not really want the position. Imbinali carried the name of the chief and acted as the leader in war, pig-killing, and ceremonies, but his uncle continued to manage the daily affairs of the village.

It was traditional for a new chief to tear down the old chief's *Poku* and build a new one, but when Imbinali took on the chief's role, he did not want to build a *Poku* because he said that too often it was used for trouble and death. Tunoli built one instead. He looked after the village business while Imbinali took on a wider role in the valley.

Imbinali often found himself thinking differently from his clansmen and did not want to participate in many practices of the surrounding tribes. Lendepame's nephew, Koke Itua, often came to visit, and the two men found themselves drawn to each other. Both had fathers who were fearsome warrior chiefs with many wives, yet for some reason that they did not understand themselves, Imbinali and Koke did not want to follow in their fathers' ways. They thought there must be a better way, and they spent many hours talking and dreaming together.

One thing Imbinali and Koke Itua never taught their children was the ways of cannibalism. The elders of their villages took great pride in telling people that cannibalism was not practiced in their tribes, and they warned the children about dangers beyond their valley.

From the time Nombo was born, he heard stories about the Yambiri tribe who lived beyond the Yalo River in Puluparu. The people of Puluparu were said to be wild and their lands were places of constant bloodshed. Nombo had seen some of this fearsome tribe. They certainly looked different from his own people: they were small and thin, but their stomachs were swollen, standing out like enormous round spheres in the middle of their slight bodies. Their most distinctive feature was that they never smiled. No one in Nombo's tribe had ever seen them smile and it was rumored that the cannibals could not smile.

There were times when violence among the Yambiri people escalated, and then people from the Yambiri tribe sometimes arrived in Imbinali's village to escape from the killings. Some stayed with his tribe for several years before it was safe to return.

One day a group of about thirty cannibal men arrived in Nombo's village. As soon as the adults saw them, they called their children and told them to run and hide. The strangers came over the hill in two groups, one group calling "So!" and the other group responding "O!" in a wild singing chant, striking their bows and arrows in a fearsome war cry. They moved in a strange jumping fashion, leaping like wallabies, with their eyes moving left and right. Imbinali shouted to his children to run into the house because he knew the men were looking for children to eat.

The children were terrified. The strangers passed up and down through the village several times, continuing to leap wildly and shout "So! O!" The adults of Kalane stood outside their houses, watching silently, and standing their ground. Eventually the strangers left and the frightened children began to emerge.

There came a time when Nombo's tribe began to hear a new sound—a loud roaring which came from the distance, grew louder and then faded away. The people could not see anything, so they lay down and put their ears to the ground to hear where the noise was coming from. They couldn't work out the source, but they noticed the sound always came from the same direction and disappeared in the direction of their enemy tribes.

The clan leaders began to use the sound to their own advantage, telling their enemies, "When you hear that noise, it means we are going to attack you." It struck fear into their enemies.

One day, the roaring was extra loud over one village and all the people ran to hide in the forest. There was a terrible noise right in the middle of the village, then silence. People from miles around came running to see what had happened. Some houses had been destroyed by a huge shining grey object that had fallen from the sky and now lay on the ground. Fortunately, no one was hurt because everyone had run into the jungle.

The people were excited and decided that this round thing was a gift from the spirit world. For months men from all over the valley hacked it to pieces with their stone knives. They discovered that pieces of this strange metal made excellent axe-heads. Years later, they learned that the strange roaring had been made by airplanes, and that the shining object was an unexploded bomb.

That was the first time they touched something from the outside world.

9

The songs of the valley

SOMETIMES THE VALLEY WAS filled with singing: songs for brides, songs for pig-killing, songs for boys becoming men. There were songs for birth and songs for death. There were songs for war and songs to celebrate peace.

The songs formed part of a rich cycle of activities in which all the daily routines of the village were seen as intertwined with the unseen spirit realm. Both worlds existed together and what happened in one world had implications in the other. When there were bouts of sickness, when the death rate was unusually high, when crops failed or even when there was strange behavior among their precious pigs, the villagers saw these events as signs of adverse activity in the spirit world.

The spiritual health of the tribe was vital in order to maintain the best possible life for the people, their animals, and their lands. The health of the forests, the soil and the rivers were seen as part of the same overall complex system: when one person or group transgressed, the whole valley suffered.

The chiefs were ultimately responsible for maintaining the health of the tribe and their lands, working together with other experts in the things of the spirit. They maintained the rituals and the cyclical festivals, and when something was wrong, they were expected to discern the problem and address it. They would not rest until they had identified the problem: it could be a moral sin like adultery, which was forbidden in the tribe, or a failure to attend to something important such as honoring a dead relative in the correct way. Whatever the trouble was, the solution usually involved action by the individual or the community to right the immediate wrong, to pay compensation, and to attend to the deeper spiritual problem.

Occasionally there were outbreaks of leprosy. Lepers had to leave the village and hide far away in the bush with other lepers. They built their own houses and gardens and everyone else knew they must not go there. Two special caves were reserved for the bodies of lepers who died.

Mount Ialibu was the most sacred place in their region and usually only the chiefs and leaders went there. Lendepame's father once had a dream on Mount Ialibu about his daughter: he saw a vision of a "half pig" (sea lion) with a beard like a man, surrounded by children eating all kinds of different food. Later, when Lendepame married, her father told her about the dream, saying, "You will always have enough food for your family. You will all be strong and healthy."

No one doubted such dreams. They believed they came from the God beyond the clouds and that He was guiding them through their lives.

Approaching the spirit realm on Mount Ialibu was not something to be taken lightly. A chief only dared to go there if he held the right authority and was morally clean. Sometimes a man would stay at the foot of Mount Ialibu for some time to prepare himself before going further.

Some local mountains were also sacred. Each village had its own special small mountain or hill where men could go to receive personal or domestic visions. Venturing to approach these mountains was a serious business. Nombo and his friends in the village of Kalane often watched their fathers and uncles preparing to go to their village's sacred mountain, Kiala. The children knew they must not follow since only initiated men could undertake the journey.

When men returned from these experiences, usually they said very little. Occasionally there was a story to tell. Once one of Imbinali's uncles, Yapamari, spent several days on Kiala and came back with a story which gripped everyone's imagination so strongly that it became part of their cycle of legends.

On Kiala, Yapamari had a dream. He saw a snake that was very colorful. It was just like one of the normal local snakes, but it was very bright, as if it had a rainbow all over its body. He saw a spear go into the snake's body, just behind its head, but the snake did not die. It was still alive, looking up at him with bright unblinking eyes. Yapamari kept watching the snake, and then he saw his brother, the chief, remove the spear from the snake's body. The snake looked up at the chief and said, "Thank you."

Yapamari knew this vision was for his tribe, so he waited on the mountain until he understood its meaning. Then he returned to the village and told them the story and the interpretation: "Every time we fight, arrows or spears will come at our legs or the back of our bodies. They will strike us and pierce us, but we will pull them out and we will survive."

This dream became part of the collection of stories which gave their tribe its identity, and it emboldened the warriors, diminishing their fear of death. Their warriors gained a reputation for survival even when they were injured; many men who were speared or shot lived to tell the tale of how they pulled out the spear or arrow, and were able to continue fighting and walk home from the battle. Dreams and visions such as this, stored in the collective memory, contributed to the tribe's sense of meaning and significance, linking their story to the larger, unseen world.

ALTHOUGH THE CHIEFS HAD their role in the spiritual life of the tribes, they were not the experts in spirit things. That position belonged to witchdoctors, mediums, and seers, who were honored and feared in equal measure. These men were often identified from an early age and spent a lifetime acquiring the skills and knowledge they needed to be the keepers of the spiritual health of the tribe.

Many people developed great expertise in the properties of plants, knowing which barks, leaves, herbs, or roots to use to treat a sore or sickness. They had plant preparations and remedies for just about every need in the village. Some saps could be used as glue, and were also smeared on a pig's carcass to remove the hairs before cooking. There were medicines and plants for all the practical issues of life.

Witchdoctors went into the forests and had supernatural encounters in which they believed they became connected with the spirits or demons of the forests. These spirits gave them secret knowledge of magic things, allowing the medicine men to partner with the powers of the unseen world. Nombo's great uncle was a skilled medium and witchdoctor who could "sing" certain spirits into his house. One of the boys of his clan would lead a dance outside the witchdoctor's house, drawing the spirits into his home. Then the witchdoctor spoke to these spirits as if they were old friends, using various techniques to demonstrate their presence and power.

He used to take a piece of ginger root, soft and fresh from the ground, and pierce it with a long bone needle. Then he handed it to one of the onlookers, who would do the same. The needle easily penetrated the soft flesh. Then the witchdoctor stretched out his hand and took back the ginger. In front of everyone, he spoke to it. He tried to put the needle back into the ginger root again, but the needle would no longer pierce the flesh.

The witchdoctor handed it to others, but no one could pierce the ginger. The fresh, juicy ginger root had become completely and unaccountably impenetrable.

Through demonstrations like this the witchdoctor established his authority, showing that he could communicate and partner with the spirits or demons that had power over the natural world.

When there was sickness or crop failure, or a series of unusual events in the village, the witchdoctor was expected to act. In some Highland tribes both "white" (life enhancing) and "black" (death promoting) magic were practiced routinely. In Imbinali's tribe, sorcery and witchcraft against others was actively discouraged and rarely practiced. The medicine men consulted the spirit world, but the emphasis was on protecting life.

THE KEY TO MAINTAINING well-being in the valley was maintaining the complex cycle of pig-killings and rituals. At the center of Kalane there were the *timbu yapu*, or spirit houses. *Timbu* is the Wiru for sky, so even in the name there was a link to the God beyond the clouds. The house and the things in it were colored with bright colors.

Imbinali's tribe had some customs that were unique to their part of the valley. The men prepared a special rosewood pole, several meters high, which stood in the middle of the *timbu yapu*. Woven cane hoops or rings encircled the pole, supported by long strips of cane that ran from the top to the bottom of the pole.

The men began to work at the bottom ring, decorating it with the bones of different animals. It took at least a month to complete one ring and then they would start on the next one. As the lower rings were finished, the men built wooden scaffolding and ladders so they could work higher and higher up the pole. When they were about a meter from the top, they sent out a message to the chief that it was time to prepare for the *mumu*.

Meanwhile, other men were working on *timbuwaras*. They made string from plant fiber and dyed it in various ochre colors, then wove elaborate flat animal-like figures based on patterns passed down through the generations. They would finish the *timbuwaras* at the same time as the pole. The whole structure, along with the *timbuwaras*, took up to five years to complete.

The chief had been raising pigs for several years in preparation for this event. Once he heard that the pole and *timbuwaras* were ready, he ordered the pigs to be slaughtered and the feast to be prepared. The men dug *mumu* pits, the women gathered vegetables and fires were lit. All the men, women and children prepared themselves with their finest belts, bilums, grass skirts and head-dresses. Messages were sent to chiefs and clan leaders from other tribes around, telling them about the feast and sending gifts in advance. Nothing was left to chance in the planning. The chief sent pieces of sugarcane to leaders of other villages. When the leader received the pieces, he understood exactly how many pigs would be allocated to him and his clan. Sometimes thousands of people would be involved in one feast cycle, bringing their bounty, and sharing it through complex inter-related family groups.

While the village prepared the feast, the men in the *timbu yapu* attached ropes to the enormous pole and began the difficult task of carrying it out into the village. The pole must always stay upright—it should "never sleep." The pole and the *timbuwaras* could not come out through the same door the men had used to enter the house, so the men broke a hole in the side of the house and carefully carried the sacred items out. This stage of the ceremony was known as *timbu yapu pea,* when the house was opened and the sacred things were brought out.

Men played sacred flutes to accompany the singing as other men held the pole and *timbuwaras* high and danced and sang their way through the village. Hundreds of people were waiting. Men and women joined in the dancing, sweeping backwards and forwards from one side of the village to the other. They carried the pole down the hill, dancing and singing until they reached the chief's house right in the middle of the village. The pole and *timbuwaras* stood there for about a month while people continued to celebrate.

Nombo saw that pole being prepared just once when his father took him into the house to watch the men at work. But away from the hearing of others, Imbinali told him, "Those things are not true. We are deceiving ourselves—it is all nonsense. People do this just because they want to eat meat and pigs." It was the culture and custom of the village, but Imbinali privately said, "They are bringing their devil out. One day, these things will be finished."

Meanwhile, Imbinali allowed the celebrations to continue. He watched Takuame and the others dancing, but he himself never danced.

In the village there was also a circular house known as a *taba,* which was for a particular female spirit. The floor was divided down the middle, representing the two main clan groups in the area. This house held two round sacred spirit stones, the larger one representing the male spirit and the smaller one the female spirit. These stones were placed in a gourd and buried right in the center of the house, to ensure the life and health of the district.

Also, in the *taba* were the skulls of significant male ancestors, placed on the inner rim of the walls. In the center of the house was a large post where the men hung plaques and trophies made from the bones of hunted animals.

The anthropologist and linguist Dr Harland Kerr witnessed these ceremonies in Yapera's village, Poloko, in 1960. Sadly, this turned out to be the last time the Spirit Pole cycle ever took place. A u-shaped long house was built for the occasion, to accommodate everyone from the three clan groups that made up Yapera's tribe. Each family had their own section, with Yapera and his family in the center. This was the only time when men, women and children lived under one roof. Every family brought food, spreading their contributions out on display.

Each clan had prepared their own spirit pole, and at the climax of the celebrations, men from each clan brought their poles and set up them in a line, in the middle of Yapera's village. This took place at the summer equinox, when the sun was directly overhead and there were no shadows.

Groups of male and female dancers performed, the men dressed as women and the women dressed as men. Dr Kerr interpreted that this signified the breaking down of normal social divisions.

The songs that were sung during celebrations all had particular significance. Each village had its own special songs reflecting the character and the priorities of the people. Lendepame and the women sang about their springs and rivers, mountains, hills, and gardens:

> *The river brings good things,*
> *The river brings life.*
> *The river is a woman,*
> *The garden also is a woman.*
> *The waters of a river*
> *Bring fish and refreshment,*
> *The garden produces fruit.*
> *The woman, the rivers, and the gardens*
> *Are the source of life.*

If a girl was interested in a boy, she and her friends would go to that boy's village and sing. They would sing a description of the pandanus garden or land of that boy, so everyone would know who they wanted. If the boy's family was not interested, they would approach the girls with a gift, saying thank you but telling them the boy was already marked for someone else.

Imbinali's village also sang about wars and strength. The men would sing about their mountain, Kiala:

> *You see that mountain—that is how strong we are.*
> *We, our clan—we have won the victory.*
> *We have won the battle,*
> *Now you must respect us.*

This was a song of celebration for times of pig-killing, when the leaders made plans for feasting and wars, and allied tribes would come and listen to the songs. There were strict rules of courtesy. One tribe would sing about their plans while the other tribes listened carefully to the words. Then they would reply in song, either promising or refusing their support. Plans were not made directly in conversation but were declared in song.

Sometimes girls would come to their male cousins' villages and sing— they would sing for the men's legs or their muscles, meaning "You are now full grown and powerful." It was an invitation for their cousins to offer gifts. The cousins would give gifts to the girls and then the girls would return home, satisfied that their clan was strong and could provide for them all.

In the spirit houses there were special chants or *leiwiyaro* which were recited by the elders to assert the tribe and its identity. They sang the list of every significant male ancestor, mentioning the names in a fixed order. They sang the names of every named site in the district: every place that had been farmed or lived in by the tribe, even if it had been abandoned and had reverted to bush. They sang the names of every type of domestic pig and cultivated crop, naming each variety. Finally, they sang the line of places from which, according to legend, their peoples and ceremonies had migrated into the Wiru. The men sang these songs to preserve their story and identity, to reaffirm their claim to their lands and to pass on that knowledge to their children.

As a young child Nombo was not allowed to enter the men's house. But he often stood outside with the women and children to listen to the songs. The men usually sang in Wiru or Kewapi, the different languages of their clans, but sometimes they sang in an older language the children did not understand.

The village celebrations honored the "small" gods, the spirits that affected the daily life of the tribes, but the people often mentioned the bigger

God, Akolali. If someone was trying to cross a flooded river and narrowly escaped death, he would say, "Akolali saved me." If a tree nearly fell on him, he would go to the medicine man or priest and say, "Please say thank you to Akolali for me."

If there was a lightning strike, people thought it was a sign from Akolali that something was not right in the village. Perhaps someone had brought poison or was using sorcery, so Akolali was not happy. If it happened repeatedly, then that village would become known as a place of trouble.

The link between the individual and Akolali was very strong. In the Wiru language there was a word, *po*, meaning a line, twine, rattan, string, or vine. But it had another meaning which was even more powerful: it signified the lifeline of every person, the lifeline which Akolali held for each man, woman, and child, until Akolali himself decided it was time to snap the line. Every person in the valley knew the value of life and the closeness of death.

One day Nombo was with his father in the forest and they heard voices they believed were spirit voices. This was not unusual—many of the Highland people were familiar with spirit voices among the birds, animals, and trees. Imbinali raised his hunting spear and shouted back to the voices, "You speak boldly now. But there is a higher God who lives beyond the clouds, and one day you must bow your knee to Him!"

Nombo was puzzled. "Why do you say that? Why are you speaking to these spirits?"

His father replied, "There is another God. My son, these spirits, they are small things."

Imbinali still said nothing to Nombo about the encounter with God on the mountain, but he kept his son away from many of the rituals of their tribe. Imbinali was looking ahead, sensing that one day there would be a new cycle of songs in the valley.

PART 2

White men's tribes

10

The smell of possum and Johnson's baby powder

ALL THE PEOPLE IN the valley had a keen sense of smell. Even young children could sniff the air and know if a possum or a pig had gone by. They could tell whether the animal had been there an hour ago or the previous day, and they could often smell things from two or three miles away.

When Nombo's family were living in Tindua, they were outside their house one day when they suddenly smelled a new smell—a strange smell unlike anything they had known before. Clearly something was coming, but they had no idea who or what it was. Lendepame gathered her children and they ran into their house among their pigs, holding and patting them to keep them quiet.

The smell became thick, and there was a loud knock as if something like a stick had struck the house. The pigs jumped in fright, but Lendepame and the family all calmed them and they did not make a sound. The smell faded and eventually Lendepame and the family went outside.

They discovered huge prints on the ground, strange bold footprints with no toes. They put their own feet on those prints, and thought it must have been giants that had passed through.

Later they learned that people in other places had had the same experience. They asked each other, "Did you see them?"

Some had seen the back of the creatures. They seemed like men, but their skin was a different color. No one knew what they were, so the villages soon forgot about them.

Who were these visitors? We do not know exactly, but they were probably two patrol officers, making their first explorations through the area. Stories began to spread of men with pale skins who were walking through their lands.

Nombo's family felt unsafe after that and they moved further down the valley, away from the places where these strangers had been. They built a new village called Kolaipo in the jungle where they thought they would be hidden. Soon they heard that white men had moved into the nearby village of Ialibu, and armed native policemen from coastal areas began to pass through the villages. The native police told the clan leaders that white men had established a "station" in Ialibu, but white men were not allowed to enter Pangia yet.

Imbinali's family continued to hear about white men living nearby. Eventually the white men started living among Lendepame's tribe and some of her relatives began to work with them, helping to build a road. One day Lendepame decided to take some vegetables and sweet potatoes to her family who were working with the white men. She told Imbinali and her sons to stay in the village and she set off with Takuame.

Imbinali told his sons that while the women were away, he would teach them how to build a fence for the pigs. They worked for a while, then Neri whispered, "I want to go and see the white men. Let's go!" Nombo was excited at the idea, and the two boys waited until their father wasn't looking and slipped away from their work.

They had run at least half a kilometer when they heard their father's voice behind them. "Who has run away from me? You can't go and see the white men. They might take you."

Nombo hid in some bushes, but he was shaking so much that the leaves around him were shaking too. Imbinali saw him but ran past until he caught up with Neri. He grabbed Neri and hit him with a stick, then brought him back. Imbinali came and took hold of Nombo as well. "I already saw your tracks, but I could see that you were hiding so I got your brother first," he said.

Imbinali took the boys home to finish the fence. He stood near them holding a cane, warning them, "You make sure you do it properly." He was very upset. "You have wasted my time. Why did you want to see the white men? We don't know anything about them. I don't want to lose you."

The boys tried to build the fence, but Nombo's hands were too small to pull the cane strips tight. Imbinali watched them, hitting their hands from time to time with the cane when they did not do it properly. It was still early morning and their hands hurt in the cold air. Eventually Imbinali said, "Now let me finish it." He showed them what to do and they watched as his strong skilled hands completed the work.

Later that day they were all resting when they saw one of Lendepame's brothers, Keme, coming. The boys feared him because his face was hard and he was fierce and dangerous. He always carried two cassowary bone spears, one at each side, with possum skins hanging from them. He used to terrify people and take their belongings, so when Nombo and Neri saw him coming, they ran to hide. They watched their tall uncle go into their garden and help himself to some of their sweet potatoes. Imbinali did not challenge him because he was a relative and they were living on Lendepame's family lands. But Imbinali was upset, because it was not right to take food from someone else's garden without permission.

Later Imbinali told his family, "I think it is time to move back to Kalane to our own lands." So, they gathered their pigs and belongings and sent word to all the young men from their clan to come and help. Early in the morning they set out and carried everything back to Kalane. They repaired their village and were happy to be back in their own lands.

A few months later, Nombo was with his family in the gardens when two white men appeared. The children and adults said nothing, but they were terrified. Most of them had never seen white men before. They all stood still, their eyes to the ground. They thought it was their ancestors coming back: they believed that when people died, they changed their color. They did not want to look at them or touch them and soon the white men walked away.[2]

White men kept appearing after that. An anthropologist and linguist called Dr Harland Kerr arrived with his wife Marie and their baby daughter Bronwyn, and settled across the valley in Yapera's village of Bolona. Lutheran missionaries and Catholic priests came, as well as government patrol officers. They all had the same smell, and all were equally unnerving to the village people.

One day a Catholic priest called Father Garry arrived in Kalane. The priest stretched out his hand and Imbinali grasped it. That was the first time anyone from Imbinali's tribe had touched a white man.

Imbinali and the other chiefs were accustomed to engaging with other tribes. For hundreds of years, the tribes had interacted with each other

---

2. Later they learned the day of the garden encounter was 16 September 1960.

through trade and exchanges, and they knew how to face the threat of battle or invasion by different groups. The tribal system remained basically intact until the coming of the white men. Their arrival marked the beginning of a different kind of interaction, with unprecedented consequences.

From the moment the strange smell entered Nombo's valley, his world began to change. Years afterwards, I asked Nombo how he would describe the smell. He thought for a minute. "It was a bit like a mixture of possum and Johnson's baby powder."

So, who were these white men coming into their valley, and why did their arrival have such an impact? To find out, we need to look at what had been happening in the outside world. Although the people of the Wiru valley did not know it, white men had already been arriving in Papua and New Guinea for over two hundred years.

11

Half devil and half child

THE FIRST EUROPEANS CAME to Papua and New Guinea for a wide variety of reasons. Some were searching for wealth and resources, others for power. It was the age of exploration, and curious explorers and adventurers were spreading across the world.

The Pacific region was popular with treasure hunters seeking gold, precious stones, new lands, and exotic creatures. Some saw New Guinea as a paradise while others saw it as a place of primitive darkness: "A rugged and mountainous country, and a race of the most savage and ruthless character."[3]

The Portuguese explorer Ferdinand Magellan landed on the mainland in 1522 and took back to Europe five birds of paradise, dried specimens purchased from the indigenous people. When the birds arrived in Europe, they were a sensation. The enraptured Europeans declared they must be birds of the gods, coming straight from Paradise.

These birds were highly prized in New Guinea as items of trade, and their legs and wings were removed before the flattened head, body and tail were dried out. Not realizing this, Europeans made up all kinds of stories. The birds were said to float high above the earth, feeding only on the dew of heaven and never coming to the ground to eat or rest. Humans only saw them when they died and fell to the ground.[4] One bird was brought to the court of the French king, and royalty elsewhere, including Charles I of the United Kingdom, asked for birds of paradise to be included in their portraits.

3. Attenborough & Fuller, *Drawn from Paradise*, 28.
4. Attenborough & Fuller, *Drawn from Paradise*, 28.

Other explorers followed throughout the sixteenth and seventeenth centuries, returning to Europe with stories of cannibals and monsters. Most preferred to observe the islands of New Guinea from the safety of their ships and only landed to get fresh water or food. They had little contact with the people.

The Dutch arrived in 1615 and the British in 1699, mapping the coastlines. A Dutch captain called Jacob Weyland picked up several New Guinean people and took them back to Amsterdam—presumably without their consent, since they had no common language. These men were the first New Guineans to set foot in Europe, and ethnologists were excited about these new human "specimens." We can only imagine their shock and bewilderment, and, sadly, there is no record of what became of them.

The first Americans who arrived in New Guinea were whalers in 1799. A whaler called Captain Morell sent home highly exaggerated stories about flocks of hundreds of birds of paradise flying from island to island and many volcanos erupting along the coasts. He kidnapped several people and took them to be exhibited in the United States.[5] There was a fashion at this time for "human zoos" which displayed exotic people from around the world.

At this time theories about different races were being debated in Europe. It was widely believed that there were "superior" races, which were lighter in color and more civilized; the darker, more "primitive" races were described as "inferior." The theory of evolution was becoming popular and many scientists suggested that the primitive races were at an earlier stage of human development. Some of their opponents, who believed in the biblical view of creation, taught that the primitive races had fallen further from the original "Adam" created by God. This meant that in both scientific and religious circles, white people regarded themselves as superior.

Perhaps the most dangerous consequence of these beliefs was that most Europeans assumed that "inferior" black races should give way to "superior" white ones. These ideas shaped the thinking and actions of many of the first white people in Papua and New Guinea. Scientists were fascinated by the birds of paradise but saw the human inhabitants of New Guinea as "most savage and ruthless in character. In those trackless wilds the birds of paradise display that exquisite beauty, calculated to excite admiration and astonishment among the most civilized and most intellectual races of man."[6]

---

5. Ballard, *The Art of Encounter*, 21.
6. Wallace, *The Malay Archipelago*, 8.

With astonishing arrogance, some Europeans believed that the beauty of the birds of paradise could only be appreciated by "civilized people." The English naturalist Alfred Russel Wallace wrote:

> I thought of the long ages of the past, during which the successive generations of this little creature had run their course—year by year being born, and living and dying amid these dark and gloomy woods, with no intelligent eye to gaze upon their loveliness; to all appearance such a wanton waste of beauty. It seems sad, that on the one hand such exquisite creatures should live out their lives and exhibit their charms only in these wild inhospitable regions, doomed for ages yet to come to hopeless barbarism; while on the other hand, should civilised man ever reach these distant lands and bring moral, intellectual and physical light into the recesses of these virgin forests, we may be sure that he will so disturb the nicely-balanced relations of nature whose wonderful structure and beauty he alone is fitted to appreciate and enjoy.[7]

Not all white men thought the same way, but when Europeans talked about the people of New Guinea, the same words kept coming up again and again: savage, unintelligent, barbaric, primitive, uncivilized, and intellectually, physically, and morally inferior. These were the assumptions in many European minds.

The lands of New Guinea were seen as "the last unknown." By the nineteenth century every continent had been explored, but Europeans were only just beginning to move into the interior of New Guinea.

The Dutch claimed the western part of New Guinea in 1828, and then in 1884 the German government claimed the north-east quarter, naming it Kaiser-Wilhelmsland. Three days later the British government declared the south-east quarter a protectorate, establishing a capital at Port Moresby. Very few of the people of New Guinea were aware of these claims. In 1845, James Dredge, former Assistant Protector to the Aborigines of New South Wales, wrote about the indigenous people of Australia:

> Although they have been taken under the British power, it is entirely without their knowledge and concurrence. No wonder they have failed to appreciate the privilege. Hence, they adhere to, and consider themselves justified in, the use of their ancient customs.[8]

The same could have been said about the people of New Guinea.

7. Wallace, *The Malay Archipelago*, 233.
8. Dredge, *Brief Notices of the Aborigines of New South Wales*, 67.

Part 2 | White men's tribes

In 1901, Australia was given the responsibility for British New Guinea, which was renamed Papua Territory. When World War 1 broke out, Australian troops moved into German New Guinea, and by September 1914 the German forces had surrendered. Now the eastern half of the mainland came under Australian authority.

Europeans established plantations, which removed a whole generation of young men from their families and villages. The men could no longer participate in the gardening, fishing, hunting and cultural life of their communities. In many coastal areas, the men's houses fell into disrepair. By 1920 about one thousand white people were living in New Guinea, mostly men. Governor John Hubert Murray was aware of some of the issues and appointed a government anthropologist, who he hoped would improve understanding of indigenous cultures and attitudes:

> I expect from the anthropologist no less a result than the bridging of the gulf which separates the Stone Age from the twentieth century, and the passage of which has cost so much suffering to primitive races.[9]

The most notable anthropologist was F.E. Williams, who spent twenty years in Papua travelling, photographing, and documenting people and places. Like Governor Murray, Williams believed that the administration's priority was the protection and promotion of indigenous interests, but they were always outsiders looking at a society that was profoundly different from their own.

Murray stated more than once: "Tribal chiefs practically do not exist in Papua."[10] This reiterated the view of the earliest missionaries such as the Reverend Samuel McFarlane of the London Missionary Society, who likewise did not see evidence of authority structures, and commented on the "absence of powerful chiefs. In New Guinea there are no real chiefs, but headmen, who are leaders in time of war, but have little influence or power in times of peace beyond their own families."[11]

Interestingly this view still existed in the 1950s, when instructions issued to Australian patrol officers stated: "In nearly every part of Papua and New Guinea, we are faced with the problem that there is no hereditary

---

9. Young & Clark, *An Anthropologist in Papua*, 7.
10. Murray, *Papua or British New Guinea*, 25.
11. McFarlane, *Among the Cannibals*, 28.

chieftainship and scarcely any framework upon which to hang parallel forms of introduced lawful controls and supporting authority.[12]

This is quite baffling from a Papua New Guinean perspective, since the system of tribes and chiefs was what held their society together. Perhaps the early colonizers were more accustomed to the chiefs and leaders elsewhere, with more obvious outward trappings and despotic authority, so the white men may have missed the more unobtrusive complexities of the chief system in Papua and New Guinea. It may explain the way the white men dealt with chiefs such as Imbinali when they finally entered the Highlands. One patrol officer from early days in the Wiru valley showed us an old photograph which he described as "two local fellows." When a local man saw the same photo, he immediately recognized that one of the "local fellows" was a chief, and one a newly initiated man. The newly initiated man wore a headband of white shells, while the chief had leather bands around his legs. To white eyes, the markings of a chief were invisible. Imbinali and many of his peers tended to conduct themselves quite democratically, leading through discussion and consensus rather than by force.

The Australians saw their role as protection, but racism was deeply rooted in their thinking. In 1945, a member of the Australian Parliament made this comment in a debate: "The native psychology and mentality are entirely different from that of the European. The boy [indigenous man] is half-devil and half-child, who has the mentality of a child about eight years old."[13] The idea that black Papuans were inferior to the point of being mentally deficient was so normal that it could be expressed openly in the Australian Parliament without causing dismay. The description of an indigenous person as "half-devil and half-child" comes from a poem by Rudyard Kipling, "The White Man's Burden." White men felt they had a responsibility to bring peace, freedom, and prosperity to their "new-caught, sullen peoples, half-devil and half-child."

We cannot judge the past in the light of the present, but such attitudes had a profound effect on the peoples of Papua and New Guinea.

MEANWHILE, SINCE 1871, ANOTHER group of people had also been arriving in New Guinea—the missionaries.

From the beginning the role of the missionaries was different. They were interested in the people rather than the land or resources:

---

12. *Circular Instruction No. 147*, 1.
13. Nelson, Lutton & Robertson, *Select Topics in the History of Papua New Guinea*, 39.

> It was not the treasures of the country, but the inhabitants we sought—the multitude of souls who have lost the image of God which Jesus Christ, whose gospel we are commanded to preach, came to restore. We are fully convinced that this gospel is the only means for preventing the natives from being swept from the face of the earth by the great tidal wave of what we are pleased to call "human progress and civilization."[14]

Missionaries around the world had seen the path of "progress" and they knew that the sudden influx of Europeans would have a devastating effect on the inhabitants. The earliest missionaries saw themselves as standing on the side of the indigenous peoples, and they lived among them and learned the local languages as quickly as possible.

Perhaps it is not surprising that the missionaries were the first to describe the people of New Guinea positively. Samuel McFarlane wrote:

> I can testify to the possession of many noble qualities by the cannibals. They are not deficient in courage, manliness, and even humanity, as some people foolishly declare them to be; and they are even distinguished for their hospitality. Indeed, they are as a rule a good-tempered, liberal people—greatly superior in these qualities to their lighter colored neighbors who look down upon them.[15]

McFarlane summarized the prevailing attitudes of the late 1800s:

> We all doubtless believe that we belong to one of the most civilized nations on the face of the earth; that we have made and are still making wonderful progress, and look down upon savages (some with pity, others with contempt, and many with indifference) as being far below us. Yet few seriously consider what is the ideally perfect social state?[16]

He must have shocked many with his conclusion:

> Some say that it is to be found in one part, and some in another of Christendom. And yet I do not hesitate to say that I have found the natives in the South Seas and in New Guinea, in their low state of civilization, approaching nearer that ideal perfect social state.

His reasons for this view included the lack of focus on material wealth, the comparative equality within New Guinea society and the democratic

14. McFarlane, *Among the Cannibals*, 24.
15. McFarlane, *Among the Cannibals*, 103–4.
16. MacFarlane, *Among the Cannibals*, 129–30.

decision-making processes within villages, all of which he contrasted with contemporary British society.

The missionaries were keen observers and critics of the degradation caused by the first interactions between white men and the indigenous inhabitants:

> Their spirits are humiliated by a sense of inferiority. In savage life they were gentlemen, as far as having the means to supply their wants goes to make a gentleman. Luxury [now] spreads its ample board before their eyes, but they are excluded from the banquet.[17]

The missionaries spoke with the voice of long experience about the destructive effects of "civilization":

> What we are pleased to term civilization generally begins in despotism, or, I might even say, in murder and plunder. A country is seized, the land appropriated, and the natives subdued, and placed under laws. Then, as education advances, and the subdued begin to feel their power, the struggle begins, and goes on for ages, between radicals and conservatives; the one trying to regain the rights and liberties of their fathers, and the other trying to retain what was gained by conquest. All I can say is, that I devoutly hope that New Guinea may be preserved from such civilizing influences.[18]

Sadly, the voices of these missionaries were largely unheard and the drive to explore, claim and plunder New Guinea continued.

Missionaries gradually spread across the land, spreading a new message about a God who has a son called Jesus and who speaks through a special book. The missionaries sent by SIL (Summer Institute of Linguistics) and Wycliffe Translators were trained linguists and spent years learning local languages, then developing their first written forms. They were the first people to bring literacy to Papua New Guinea, and they continue to play a vital role in documenting and preserving the country's languages today.

Missionaries were also the first to establish schools, medical clinics, and communications in most of the country. Unlike government workers or traders, who tended to come and go, the missionaries lived among the local people for years, building up relationships and gaining a level of trust.

This is just a glimpse of what had been going on outside Nombo's valley. So, when the first white men moved in, they were not just isolated

---

17. MacFarlane, *Among the Cannibals*, 131.
18. MacFarlane, *Among the Cannibals*, 136.

individuals passing through. These white men carried with them the weight of governments and worldviews from different continents, and they believed they had the right to take control of Nombo's world without the local people's consent.

12

Nombo goes to school

WHEN NOMBO WAS FIVE years old, his cousin Amba came to stay with them for a few days. Amba was the son of Keme, Lendepame's fierce brother who had stolen their sweet potatoes. Amba told Nombo that there was a school in Tindua and that he and some others from his village had been going there every morning. He said Nombo could come too.

They did not tell Nombo's parents about it, but early the next morning, when everyone in the village had gone to their gardens, he and Amba set off for Tindua. It took nearly all day to walk there. Nombo slept at Amba's house overnight and in the morning, they went to school.

The school was a simple bush materials building, open on two sides, with dried grasses spread on the ground. The boys went inside and sat down. A white man was standing at the front, and Nombo watched him and waited to hear what he would say. The man began to speak. Nombo glanced around at the other children, who were all looking everywhere and not listening. The man was speaking Pidgin, which none of the boys knew.

Nombo turned to his cousin to find out what was going on. Amba whispered, "This is school. This is what happens in a school, you know."

Nombo did not know, but he watched the man as he continued to speak strange words. Then the teacher told the boys to close their eyes, demonstrating what to do.

Nombo whispered to his cousin, "Why are we closing our eyes?"

"This is school. This is what happens in a school."

It was the answer to everything. So Nombo closed his eyes too, and the man said more strange words, followed by a loud "Amen!" Eventually the man stopped speaking and the boys ran home.

Nombo and Amba talked all night about this thing called school. Amba said that one day the white men would take them all to a school far away. Nombo said that was okay.

They went back the next day and the same things happened. On the third day, Nombo decided he should start listening more carefully so he could learn to understand what the man was saying. He started to follow a few of the instructions: sit down, stand up, come. And always the strange custom of everyone closing their eyes and then the man saying "Amen."

Nombo kept questioning his cousin. "Why do we go to school?"

"So that we can be like white men."

"Oh! Are we going to change our color and become white?"

"I don't know."

On the fourth day, Nombo was sitting in school when a boy touched his arm and whispered, "Your dad is outside."

The teacher saw Imbinali and went outside to speak to him. He came back and asked, "Is someone called Nombo here?"

Amba was scared of his uncle and cowered down, hoping the chief would not see him. Nombo stood up and went out to his father.

"What are you doing here?" Imbinali asked.

"This is a school where we can learn to be like white men." Nombo tried to sound bold but he was scared.

"There are three things wrong with this. First, you might get poisoned. We don't know anything about these white men. Second, you didn't ask me if you could come. I don't like that. Third, you are not old enough yet. I am going to take you back home."

"I want to stay."

Imbinali was not pleased. "You are a chief's son. You must be especially careful."

So Nombo went home with his father.

One day two Lutheran missionaries arrived in Kalane. They wanted to establish the Lutheran faith in the village, but Imbinali happened to be away that day and the clan did not want to make any decisions without him. A week later, two different men came and explained they were Catholic missionaries. They said the other missionaries were Lutherans who followed a man from Germany called Martin Luther. The priests said they belonged to the Catholic Church, which was based in Rome and was very big and very strong.

Imbinali listened to them and felt he wanted to follow the Catholic missionaries. He called the clan leaders together to discuss the matter and they decided to receive the Catholic missionaries and give them some land. Imbinali suggested they give their fighting land to the priests to show that tribal wars were over. The other leaders agreed. Before long the priests began to build on the fighting land, which stood between Imbinali's tribe and the tribes who used to be their enemies.

Nombo never forgot the day Father Garry came and stood in front of the *Poku Wiru*. The first thing the priest did was to put a bright red rubber ball on the ground. The whole village gathered round to see what it was. He showed the children how to kick it. The adults and children went wild with excitement as he told them about soccer, communicating in a mixture of Pidgin, Wiru, and sign language. The children began to kick the ball, and then the priest took it, running and dribbling it around the children. No one went to work that day or the next because they were all having so much fun playing with the ball.

On the third day, a child kicked the ball into someone's house. The family were annoyed and threw it outside. Then another child kicked the ball and it hit a small child on the head. The child cried and its mother was angry. By now the whole village was getting annoyed at the disruption to their life, so they told the children they could not play soccer in the village any more. Father Garry agreed and helped them find a place to make a playing field.

The priests gave Imbinali and the clan leaders gifts of axes, salt, paints, and beads. Father Garry told them, "You are all Catholics now," and gave everyone little medals showing crucifixes or images of saints. He told the mothers to make strings so they could hang the medals around their necks. That was how the people of Imbinali's village became Catholics. Some other clans decided to become Catholics too, but the people of Lendepame's tribe in Tindua decided to become Lutherans. At that time none of the village people thought much about God in all these happenings.

The priests said the boys should go to school. They told Imbinali they wanted to take his eldest son, Neri, to the larger town of Mendi so that Neri could teach them the Wiru language. Imbinali agreed and told Neri he must go. Neri left home, and he and a group of other boys from different tribes all went to Mendi and received an education there, learning to become skilled translators.

The priests also said Nombo and the other young children should start school in the village. Imbinali and his men helped the priests to clear land at Maiyereke, near the border of their tribal lands. The villagers erected a bush materials building to be used as a church and classroom. Imbinali placed the school on the border between his tribe and their enemies because he wanted the children of both tribes to go to school together and become friends.

Nombo and many of the local children, both boys and girls, began to go to school, walking there every morning. They spent two years learning to speak and understand Pidgin. At first it was difficult, but Nombo was excited to learn Pidgin and then the alphabet.

The boys wore little—just bark belts and woven bilums in front, with long tanget leaves hanging at the back. Like small boys everywhere, mischief was never far away. When they had to sit still for long periods of time, their favorite diversion was tying together the tanget leaves of the two boys sitting in front of them. There was much subdued excitement as they waited for the moment when the boys tried to stand up, then hilarity when they fell over.

One day when Nombo was on his way to school, a man came up to him and gave him a piece of sugarcane. Nombo took it and was about to chew on it. Suddenly he remembered his father saying, "If someone you don't know gives you something to eat, don't take it. It may be poisoned. There is one way to tell: if you throw away something that is poisoned, there will be a landslide in that place."

Nombo held the sugarcane and studied the man out of the corner of his eye. The man was still watching him. Nombo ran off into the grassland and ducked down so the man could not see him, and he threw the sugarcane away. Then he ran as fast as he could to school.

He forgot about the incident and did not tell his father until a year later. His father stared at him. "Where you threw that sugarcane—everyone has been complaining about a big landslide there. No one could understand it because it is not a steep hill and there seemed no reason for a landslide. You should have told us earlier."

Nombo never forgot that. Later Imbinali discovered that another boy had been poisoned and died about the same time. The landslide is still there to this day.

NOMBO GOES TO SCHOOL

Father Garry found Imbinali's tribe surprisingly open to the Christian message. Government workers and anthropologists also noticed that the Wiru people were "more receptive to change than many other places in the Highlands. People were eager to give up their old ways and embrace the new."[19]

Imbinali had already been seeking new ways, and he hated the tribal fighting. He treasured his sons and wanted change so his children could grow up in safety. Other tribal leaders in the valley were influenced by him: they were tired of sleepless nights when they had to be constantly alert to danger. They too were ready to listen to new ideas. And of course, Imbinali and Koke Itua had already met this new God on Mount Ialibu.

When Nombo was about nine years old, the priests began a new primary school at Yareporoi, near Pangia. Pangia was now known as "Pangia Station" because the Australian patrol post had been established there and it was becoming the administrative center for the region. The priests asked Imbinali if Nombo could go there.

For Nombo it was a strange experience. Instead of living in the women's house with his mother and brothers, he now lived at the school in a house with twenty boys. The school was about seven kilometers from Nombo's village, so the boys only went home on Fridays and had to walk back to school on Monday morning. Because he was slightly older than most of the other boys, he was put in charge of them.

The students all slept together in one large hut with woven bamboo walls and a thatched roof. It was cold at night, so they all huddled together under their blankets on the bamboo floor. Nombo later remembered those times as difficult. As is natural with so many small children, most nights one or more wet the bed, so it was not unusual for the boys to be sleeping with wet and smelly blankets. Some of the little boys cried at night because they wanted their mothers.

The boys were largely left to their own devices. The priests gave them supplies of greens and sweet potatoes and showed them how to cook the food over a fire. The boys ate the vegetables and drank the soupy water. They each cooked their own food, sometimes cooperating but often competing for firewood and space. The boys had to find their own firewood, and when the priests threw away large tins from their tinned food, the boys fought for them to use as cooking pots.

---

19. Strathern, *Social Change in Pangia*, 2.

Part 2 | White men's tribes

From our perspective now, it seems harsh that small children were expected to look after themselves. However, in the context of the time it was not unusual. Young children in Papua New Guinea were much more independent and skilled than children in Western countries. Even in the 1970s some primary schools provided no accommodation for pupils from outlying areas. One man told us there had only been one primary school in his region, many miles from his village. He was so desperate for an education that at the age of six he walked all the way to the school and built himself a bush hut in the jungle nearby. He lived there completely alone, hunting for his food, maintaining his own house, and looking after himself, for the six years of his schooling. This is not an unusual story, and he does not think of himself today as having been neglected or deprived. He is now a wealthy businessman with a generous heart for the poor.

The priests kept chickens and goats and taught the boys how to look after them. At Christmas and on special occasions, they had a feast with chicken or goat meat. Sometimes Nombo led the more daring boys to creep out in the middle of the night to steal eggs from the chicken house. They were rarely caught, and these midnight raids were a highlight of their young lives, adding a spice of excitement to their sometimes tedious school days. Sometimes they confessed their sins to the priests, who forgave them and told them to say two Hail Marys and two Our Fathers.

Nombo's father had trained him well in hunting skills, and he went hunting often because the boys were hungry for protein. One of the teachers had a big German shepherd and Nombo decided to take the dog hunting with him. He found it was a quick learner and trained it to hunt. Nombo would mimic the whistle of birds and wait for their reply. The dog listened, then ran and chased the birds back towards Nombo. When the birds flew up, Nombo flung his throwing stick and usually killed them instantly. He gained a reputation among the other boys as a skilled hunter and natural leader.

The children were taught English and learned to read and write. Nombo enjoyed some aspects of school and was keen to learn, but many of the boys were homesick and found boarding life too hard. Throughout that first year, some boys ran away and returned to their homes. By the time Nombo was ten or eleven, he found himself often caring for the younger children, comforting them in their homesickness and sorting out their quarrels.

One boy in that first class was a source of envy because he wore a cloth *lap-lap* given to him by other missionaries. Eventually all the boys were given a red *lap-lap* to wear for church on Sundays. After church they had to give the *lap-lap* back to their teachers, who washed them ready for the next Sunday.

The worst thing about school was washing in the river every morning. The children from the hill villages were not used to washing or swimming in the cold rivers, so when the priests took them to wash, it was a shock. The fast flowing water was so cold that it hurt. One morning Nombo was the last to wash. He jumped into the river, but the fast current sucked him under the water. He managed to get to the surface and raise one hand, then he was pulled under again. He came up a second time and saw that just one boy was still on the bank and everyone else had gone. It was a boy called Tambran from an enemy tribe. Nombo raised his hand again, then Tambran jumped into the water and managed to drag him out.

Later Nombo thanked him for saving his life. Tambran's name meant devil, but he told Nombo, "God saved you. You have got something special in your future." Nombo never forgot Tambran's courage or his words.

Because the Catholic mission at Yareporoi had opened a year or two after the other missions there, they had to take less favored land in a flat swampy area. There were three lakes nearby, one of which was known as a "lake for lepers." Sometimes if a person with leprosy was close to death, others would take them and throw them into the lake. It seems harsh, but at that time there was no treatment for this dread disease and drastic action was taken to prevent it spreading. The local people feared and avoided this lake because it was a place of death.

One of the challenges the mission faced was superstitious fear, and this came to a head when two teachers drowned in one of the smaller lakes nearby. The boys were very upset. Many of them went to the lake with digging sticks and whatever others tools they could find, trying to break down the muddy banks so they could drain the lake where their teachers had died. But the lake kept filling with water. Eventually they gave up, saying, "The lake refused to be emptied." In fact, it was fed by an underground river so it could not be drained.

Some of the boys left the school then, or their families took them away, believing that the deaths were a sign of the spirits' disapproval of the school.

Nombo, however, stayed on and continued through primary school. And soon the little boy from the jungle, who had dreamed of being a warrior, began to wonder if God was calling him to be a priest.

13

Holy water on the spirit house and a flying angel

AS LIFE CHANGED FOR Nombo, so the world around him was also changing. Other schools were being built all over the district, new buildings were springing up, and roads and bridges were connecting people throughout the valley.

Attitudes and beliefs were also taking new directions. By the early 1960s, under the influence of the missionaries, many of the Wiru people were starting to abandon their *timbu yapu* and the spirit things.

One day the priests gathered the older children together and said that all those who had attended school faithfully were going to be baptized. It was a huge occasion, and hundreds of parents came to watch. Nombo was about ten years old and his parents agreed to come.

Father Garry sprinkled Nombo with water and said, "Your name is now changed from Nombo to Charles Nombo Lapa."

Nombo was deeply moved by the whole experience. When all the children had been baptized, the priests announced to the parents that their children now belonged to the Catholic Church. Imbinali and Lendepame were pleased and wanted to be baptized themselves.

During the holidays the priests sent the boys home to their villages. One Friday afternoon Nombo was in Kalane when the priests arrived, carrying a bottle of holy water. The priests stood outside the *timbu yapu* and said there was going to be a purification of the village. They went inside and began to pray. Nombo and the other boys followed them and watched as the priests threw holy water on the walls and the spirit objects, saying, "In the name of the Father, the Son and the Holy Spirit."

As they prayed, Nombo suddenly felt as if there was a noise like a wind and something rushed out, leaving the spirit house. He said it felt somehow different and clean. The priests led the boys through the village and did the same thing at every ceremonial and sacred place. They told the boys to get sticks and strike the old sacred places. The boys found it all very exciting and did as the priests asked. At each place the same thing happened: it was as if something rushed away and the atmosphere changed. They went around the village, claiming it for God alone.

Imbinali was delighted. "I have always known that when the big God comes, all these devils will have to go."

Others agreed, "Now there will be no more pig killing and blood for all those devils. It is all finished."

The priests went to other villages, saying in each one, "This is a purification of the village. We claim this village for God alone."

From that time, the mindset of many villages changed. The people in that area had always known that the God beyond the clouds was there; now they said He was making Himself known and they began to worship Him. Imbinali told the priests in front of his people, "We've had enough of the devil."

Soon after that the Lutheran Church set up a medical clinic in the valley. One day Nombo had an intense pain in his stomach, so his father carried him all the way to the Lutheran mission at Tiripini, near Pangia Station, the patrol officers' base. The missionary checked his eyes and stomach and gave him medicine. The mission only kept serious cases at the clinic so Imbinali had to take Nombo there every day to get more medicine. He soon recovered. That was their first experience with the white men's medicine.

Although the priests often appeared uncompromising, they were men of wisdom and keen to preserve what they could of the local ways. Father Garry promised they would do their best to protect and not destroy the people's way of life. Some other missionaries were encouraging the people to burn down their spirit houses and destroy everything to do with the old ways. The priests, on the other hand, knew that modernity would change the valley forever, so they began to collect and store away items from the villages so the memories would not be lost. They gathered weapons, headdresses and clothing, household goods and tools. They also collected items from the spirit houses: carved figures, large round stones used for divination, and *timbuwaras*, so that in years to come the children would be able to learn how their grandparents and great-grandparents used to live.

Nombo's baptism was followed by another event that touched his life forever. After he was baptized, he went home to his village on the Friday afternoon. His parents made some food and then he slept. That night he had a dream, unlike anything he had experienced before.

He dreamed that an angel came and picked him up, and he clung to it as it began to fly. The angel carried him higher and higher like an eagle until he was looking down over his valley. They flew further until he could see mountains, rivers and villages, forests, and waterfalls beyond his own valley. All night they soared through the sky together, and when Nombo awoke, he was filled with an enormous sense of awe. It seemed to him this was not just a dream—it was an encounter with God. The rapture he had experienced seemed like the very presence of God, and that feeling stayed with him throughout the day.

The next night he had the same dream, and this time they flew further, seeing more valleys and mountains, new rivers, waterfalls, and villages. Night after night he dreamed and the young boy felt he was being carried by the presence of God to see places all over the land. The joy and wonder were so strong that it pervaded his whole life. During the day Nombo saw the birds of paradise, delighting in their colors and lovely songs, and at night he felt as if paradise was with him and he was experiencing a glimpse of heaven on earth.

Nombo did not tell anyone about the dreams but he began to cultivate an inner life with God. These nightly encounters were so important to him that he decided he had to "be a good boy" and live a clean life. He believed that if he started to do bad things and disobey God, the dreams would stop. They continued for several years.

It was not until he was an adult that Nombo heard the story of how God had called his special name, Tiki, on the mountain. But from the time he began dreaming, he believed within his own heart that God was calling him and carrying him "on wings like an eagle" for a purpose. Nombo did not understand all this at the time, but loving God and living the life that God had prepared for him became the most important driving force in his life.

As he grew older the dreams stopped, but the memories lingered. Nombo believed that God had been showing him a glimpse of his nation. By the time he was a teenager, his life was filled with expectation.

14

A village of peace

WHILE THESE EVENTS WERE taking place, other missionaries were spreading throughout the Wiru valley. William and Hedwig Hertle established the Lutheran mission at Tiripini, Gene Graves led the Bible Mission at Alia, and Harland Kerr and his wife, Marie, were based in Bolona. Harland was a linguist with SIL (Summer Institute of Linguistics), and he became fluent in the Wiru language and began a translation of the Bible. He was also a keen anthropologist and observed and documented Wiru culture. Marie Kerr was a nurse, and the patrol officers kept her supplied with medicines to treat the people who lined up at her door every day. Marie also held literacy classes for adults and children, and Chief Yapera led the way in learning to read and write in just a few months.[20]

The Kerrs were surprised at how receptive Yapera was towards them. Right from the beginning he welcomed them into his village, and had a house built for them just meters away from the spirit house. Others in his clan were nervous, because they were preparing for their most important celebrations, the spirit pole ceremonies, which happened every four or five years. Some of the leaders argued that these strangers might cause trouble. But Yapera held his ground and the Kerrs were allowed to stay. Later, Yapera told Marie that before they had arrived, he had a spirit dream telling him about their coming, so when they appeared he believed that they were messengers from God. Most men and women in Yapera's village learned to read and write in less than a year, and they all converted to Christianity.

20. Kerr, *Yapeta's story from 1960*.

Dr Kerr believed that the Wiru people's own spiritual beliefs had prepared them for the message of Jesus. Their ceremony of the poles or trees, set up at the equinox, enabled the Wirus to identify with the story of the crucifixion, that moment when spiritual darkness was completely overcome by the light. Perhaps the Wiru people were not completely abandoning their old belief system, rather they were finding that essential elements of it were now being explained and fulfilled in new ways.

Another missionary, Gerald Bustin, arrived in the early 1960s representing EBM (the Evangelical Bible Mission). Soon afterwards, the quiet village of Maia, near Pangia Station, began to experience some unique events. It all began when Gerald Bustin started teaching the people of Maia to memorize the Ten Commandments. This puzzled them at first but they felt that this man had authority, and the whole village gathered every day to memorize and recite the commandments. Kakale, the oldest lady in Maia, tells her story:[21]

> I was living in a primitive age, when we did not know anything. We were living in our old ways like in the Dark Ages. Then Gerald Bustin, our missionary, came, and he taught us about the Ten Commandments. It was a mind-blowing thing because it was very new. How could we digest and observe these foreign things? How could we absorb them into our lives?
>
> It was a new thing, so it was hard for me. I was shivering, shaking. I was feeling hot but shaking as well because there was so much to take in. It was hard to open my mouth and speak about the new things. When the missionary gathered the people around, I was scared that he might ask me to speak, so I was hiding.
>
> I was hiding, but he knew my name, so he picked me and told me to speak. It was hard to learn all the commandments, so one day I learned the first commandment, the next day the second, then the third. I was constantly learning word by word and practicing, and I was the first woman to learn all the commandments.
>
> At that time, I did not understand how to pray because they had not taught us how to pray yet. Although we did not know how to pray, the Spirit of the Lord taught us. I don't know how but he just did. So, there were two things that I could do: I could pray and say the Ten Commandments. Those were the only things I knew.
>
> Because I knew those two things, Gerald Bustin told me, "Now you are able to teach others, you can teach them how to pray and

---

21. Levengo, *Private Interview*, 2013.

learn the Ten Commandments, because you are the first to do those things."

So, I began to go to people's houses and I taught my fellow village people about the Ten Commandments and I taught them how to pray. Then the missionary told us about fasting. He said that we should start to pray in the morning, before we eat, then later when the sun is right up, we can eat. We felt that the missionaries had authority, so we obeyed what they told us. We started praying every morning and didn't eat until later.

When we were praying, really into prayer, we found that we were confessing our sins. I had killed someone's dog and I confessed and repented that I had killed the dog, and I also confessed stealing a pandanus fruit. Everyone did the same, praying, and confessing things that had been hidden, exposing whatever had been covered up. When I confessed, I was overwhelmed and so excited, and I felt that I did not want to repeat the same old behaviors, stealing then covering up. I wanted to do good things. Confessing made my spirit feel free. I left the past and tried to adapt to a new way of living. Others were all experiencing the same things. Everyone was so excited.

I knew that God had changed me because some of my ways had gone and I was practicing new things. I was so happy and felt that my mind was fresh and clean.

I was married with four children. One night I was having dinner with my family, then I went to bed; and when I was lying down there was something that I could feel all over me. I could feel my spirit becoming lighter and it was as if my shoulders were growing wings. It is hard to express what I was feeling inside of me, but it was as if deep down within me I was being uplifted while I was still sleeping.

It happened every night. I told my family not to sleep close to me, because all of me was uplifted and there was a different feeling in my life. I didn't want anyone to disturb me. I felt so different at that time. There were some burdens that I used to carry deep down inside me, but at that time it was like when you take off a cloak—it was as if something was being unveiled within me. I was overwhelmed. The burdens and pains in my heart left me and I was uplifted.

Both night and day I was happy. There was something like a rushing wind, like you can see when the wind blows and you see the branches moving. Within my body it was like the same kind of wave—my body was shaken as if by a wind. I felt so light and

I felt good feelings come on me. A joyful heart was springing out of my heart.

The fire of God burned in my heart and I thanked the Holy Spirit because He chose me and burned that fire in me. I was so happy. All the good things were poured into my life and all the past burdens were gone. I can't tell you where it came from and where it goes but I could feel the power. At that time, I was the only one to have these experiences.

One morning people were preparing to go for a church service when I heard people saying that the Spirit of the Lord had fallen upon another lady called Pokeame. Her house is in the middle of the village. The Spirit of the Lord fell upon me first and then it went through her. When it was daybreak, Pokeame was filled with the Spirit of God. Many people in the village came around her house and everyone was watching her and saying that the Spirit of the Lord has come upon her too, and everyone was expecting the same Spirit that was on her to come on them. They were all waiting for the same power.

At that time people were repenting. If they had some debts, they paid back those debts, and people were obeying the Word of God. Just like me, Pokeame was happy and excited and she was telling a parable, "I was going out fishing and now you are hooked onto that bait."

When the Spirit of God came, He did not come on one person only. It started through both of us, and then it was like an outpouring in our village, so everyone who came received the same Spirit. Some of them really took it in their hearts and they accepted it and repented and lived with it for their whole lives. Others just would flow with the Spirit for a time, but they took it lightly and did not really take it into their hearts.

After that, many of us went to other villages and the same Spirit fell there. We sometimes gathered at the mission station at Mele where there were other missionaries. All those who experienced the power of God at that time went to there, together with people from all the other villages. The same Spirit of God fell on everyone there.

The missionaries were so happy to see what had happened. They recognized that the Spirit of God was being poured out and they were amazed. When people were sick, others prayed and they were healed, every time. There was such a strong belief that they would get well.

Before that time, we had a "doctor leaf" in our village. We used to rub it on our bodies when we were sick. It was a magic and healing leaf and you would get well when you rubbed on those leaves. But I left those things behind and said, "Jesus is now my healing leaf." I used to need a walking stick to walk, but I said, "Jesus is now my walking stick and I will hold onto Him. If I get ill, then I will rely on Him." I did not need my walking stick anymore because I believed that I would walk with Jesus as my guide.

After that God gave me strength. There are big rivers here, the River Polu and River Nama. We had to cross them to get to the church. Although they are huge rivers, they seemed like little creeks to me. I used to carry my little children in the bilum and hold the other children's hands to get across. It was a long distance but there was an inexpressible strength in me and I never got tired.

So, whatever we received from the Spirit of God at that time, I don't know about other people, but for myself I treasure it and keep holding onto it because it is still so special to me. I am an orphan and now a widow, very old physically, and I am not able to walk around and share the love of God with others. But I always share with fellow Christians in the church that the love of God is great, and it is so real. The Spirit of God is true. Two of my children went to be with the Lord just recently. They must be with their father—he went earlier on. I will be glad to go and meet them in heaven.

You might want to hear big stories or something tremendous that happened, but it was just like a wind that blows. People were enlightened, full of joy and laughter, and it was like a wind blowing across everyone. I didn't see where that wind comes from and where it blows to, but I just saw those things and people were happy.

People were doing things they could not do before. There was a tall pole, because we were building a large building where we could have fellowship. People were climbing up that pole as if they wanted to fly. They were swinging high up in the trees, singing and happy. People were dancing, singing, and laughing, jumping high as if they could fly. They were all climbing high and singing like birds.

Other missionaries came to see us here, and they said that it was the Spirit of God and it would break out in other places too. It seemed that the Spirit was so thick on us at that time. And it did break out in other places. The power of the Spirit of God that we were experiencing, with prayer, repentance, confession, and an outpouring of God. It happened in many other villages in the valley. It was like an outpouring of holiness over our valley.

Thank you, Father in heaven, our universal God, the God who created heaven and the earth. Your blood is so powerful, and your Spirit is so powerful. You are the great God, our Father. Oh, our Father, compared to you we are nothing.

Our faith was so strong. It felt as if heaven had literally come to earth. People were lifted, crying, dancing, praising God, confessing. All our thinking was changed. My whole body was consumed by fire and warmth. The whole valley was holding the purity of God.

Some of the missionaries told us that, in the future, a new last revival will come on us again. I am waiting for that and expecting that. We just wait on God to see what will happen.

15

Badly cooked cabbage and a kiap wants a wife

THE MISSIONARIES WERE NOT the only people making an impact. By now Australian patrol officers had arrived in the valley. What kind of men were they, and how did they go about taking charge of the district?

The first patrol post in the Southern Highlands was established in the 1930s at Lake Kutubu by Ivan and Claude Champion, and this post became a base for further exploration. Patrol posts were established in nearby areas including Erave, just beyond the Yalo River which forms the southern border of the Wiru valley. The first patrol post in the Wiru valley was established at Ialibu in 1950 and the last one at Pangia in 1961, when the whole of the Wiru valley was finally opened up to Australian administration.

The patrol officers were administrators, local governors, magistrates, and police all rolled into one. Although the official title was "patrol officer," they were popularly known as "kiaps" in many areas. The origin of the word is unknown, but it is perhaps linked to a Malaysian word for captain. Many Papua New Guinean people believed it was an Australian phrase, standing for "Keep Indigenous Always Primitive." Patrol officers told them this was not true, but the story persisted.

Their task was to make contact with the people in each district through regular patrols and to establish outposts, the objective being "the eventual pacification of the tribes to a stage when they are fit to be prepared for the basic forms of local government."[22]

---

22. *Circular Instruction No. 147*, 1.

Part 2 | White men's tribes

It is worth noting that "pacification" did not mean subduing the tribes' resistance to Australian authority: the aim was to bring an end to tribal wars. The patrol officers' task was "peaceful penetration and consolidation of Government influence. The ideal of your objective is to gain contact, to turn that contact into confidence and then to remain as a new factor in the lives of the people at their own request."[23]

Until a district had been patrolled regularly and patrol posts established, it was "restricted." This meant that no outsiders such as traders or missionaries could enter the area. This policy was in place for several reasons. It protected white people and prevented them from moving into dangerous situations, and averted unnecessary conflicts between ignorant newcomers and local tribes. The policy also protected the local people from being overrun by outsiders with varying agendas. This proved to be beneficial and prevented exploitation by different groups all vying for land or resources.

The first patrol officers posted to Pangia were two young Australians, Brian O'Neill, and Peter Barber in 1961. They were among over two thousand young men who responded to the call to go to Papua and New Guinea as patrol officers. All were between the ages of eighteen and twenty-four and usually single, and they were recruited through advertising campaigns in Australia. They came from a variety of backgrounds. Some were university graduates while others came from industry, the army, trade, or farming.

What attracted these men to come to Papua and New Guinea? For some it was an opportunity for a career or for adventure. Some came with high ideals, seeking to achieve something of value in the world. For others the reason was less high minded. One of the young patrol officers in Erave said he ended up there because of "badly cooked cabbage in the pub."

Bill Brand was the son of a farmer in the wheat growing district of western Victoria. At nineteen he was mature for his years. Like many young men in rural Australia, Bill had had to grow up quickly, looking after the family farm when his father went off to World War 2. Bill was used to hard work, but the country town of Dimboola was not exactly exciting.

One day he and three of his mates went to the local pub for a meal. Their plates were set in front of them. There was a long silence as they took in the sight of miserable meat in watery gravy and the unappetizing odor of soggy, overcooked cabbage. Then one of them said, "There's got to be more to life than this."

---

23. *Circular Instruction No. 147*, 1–2.

They got talking about what else they could do. One said he wanted to go to Antarctica. Another said he wanted to go to Papua and New Guinea. Bill had not thought about Papua and New Guinea before, but now the idea was in his head, he decided to give it a go. He and one of his mates ended up in Papua and New Guinea, another went to Antarctica. It was as simple as that.

All applicants for Papua New Guinea were screened and interviewed, then sent to the Australian School of Pacific Administration (ASOPA) in Sydney. They were trained in the principles and practices of colonial business, from administration procedures to basic anthropology. Then they were sent to Papua New Guinea for more hands-on training, learning how to build ditches or use firearms and explosives.[24] After that, they worked under experienced patrol officers in the field, and eventually, if they were considered suitable, they were entrusted with leading patrols and given the responsibility of running their own patrol posts. Generally, they were well trained and supervised, and high standards of conduct were expected.

They were given clear instructions that "conflict is to be avoided if at all possible"[25] and were trained in "the special skill and knowledge required in the task of peaceful penetration and consolidation of Government influence."[26] When patrols went to a new area, their directive was, "At first, do not attempt anything except the establishment of a friendly relationship."[27] They were to buy food, paying properly with exchange goods such as knives, axes, salt, or the popular currency of shells. In these exchanges, they were instructed to "see that the people do not leave themselves short of food for their own needs."[28] When they were establishing patrol posts and needed land, they were to lease it under terms agreed with local leaders. If people were not willing to sell food or lease out land, then the patrol officers must not press the issue. If the officers did not obey instructions, they were withdrawn from their posts and disciplined.

Of course, in practice there were wide variations in patrol officers' competence and abilities. One man who stood head and shoulders above the rest was Ivan Champion. By the time he established the patrol post at Lake Kutubu, he had already proved his worth in several major expeditions,

24. Oates, *My Story: The Making of a Young Patrol Officer*, 4.
25. *Circular Instruction No. 147*, 1.
26. *Circular Instruction No. 147*, 3.
27. *Circular Instruction No. 147*, 3.
28. *Circular Instruction No. 147*, 10.

leading large groups through new territories without a single shot being fired. Bill Brand, who trained under him, said, "Ivan was quicksilver. He could slide through an area without causing a ripple. Then someone else would go through the same places and a dozen people would end up dead." Perhaps one of the secrets of Champion's success was the respectful relationships he developed with indigenous people and his reliance on them for guidance and local knowledge.

So, when O'Neill and Barber arrived in the Wiru valley to establish a patrol post at Pangia, they were not stepping into something completely unknown. There were officers with experience in nearby Ialibu and Erave, and many other long-established posts around the Southern Highlands.

Brian O'Neill was born in Williamstown, Melbourne. He took a degree in Law before moving to Papua and New Guinea to become a patrol officer. By all accounts he did his job well.

One of his major tasks was to build an airstrip so that supplies and equipment could be airlifted in. The strip also provided access to medical help for expatriates and others in the district. There was no earthmoving equipment and limited materials, so the patrol officers had to rely on ingenuity and manpower, using "volunteers" from the local area. Bill Brand, who built a similar airstrip in the next valley, said that all they had were shovels. "By the time we had finished, the shovels were so worn down that there was only a couple of inches left of each one."[29] It was tough work, but eventually a basic airstrip was finished and planes could fly in.

O'Neill was generally friendly and well liked, and respected by the other white people in the area. He was keen to form good working relationships with the local people, particularly the leaders. He was "full of energy and enthusiasm. He was a busy man, conscientious in all that he did."[30]

Nombo and his family watched the building of the new schools and medical clinic and were intrigued by the airstrip. The children had seen aero planes flying overhead, but the sight of the first planes landing in their valley produced awe and terror in equal quantities.

Sometime later, Imbinali's family were surprised to find that Brian O'Neill had taken a girl from Lendepame's clan as his "wife." Her name was Awambo Yari. This was a new and rather unsettling development for them all as the relationship clearly did not follow the normal rules of the valley. Their feelings were mixed. On the one hand, some were pleased and

29. Brand, *Private Interview*, 2013.
30. Nalu, *The Dawning of a New Day for Ialibu*, 2.

perhaps a little proud that the newcomer had chosen one of their family. On the other hand, this was uncharted territory.

Awambo was frequently in the patrol officers' house with Brian, but when other white visitors arrived, she had to stay away or remain in the background. Soon she found she was pregnant. It was a difficult time for her and she even considered aborting the baby.[31] However, she continued her pregnancy and gave birth to a son, who became known as Peter. Within a year, Brian O'Neill moved away from the district, abandoning Awambo and the baby. It was not easy for Awambo, but she was still young and before long she married again. Her new husband took Awambo and her child into his village and became a caring father to the boy.

Peter went to the local Lutheran and government primary schools, then began his secondary education at the new high school in Ialibu. His Australian father was still living in Papua New Guinea, but Peter had no contact with him. This was a source of grief for the young boy as he often wondered about the father he had never known. Awambo tried to contact Brian several times and eventually, when Peter was fifteen years old, Brian visited them and was willing to establish a relationship with his son. By this time Brian was running a law firm in Goroka, and he took Peter back with him and sent him to high school there. It was not easy, but gradually they built up a good relationship.

Brian supported Peter through school and university, where he studied accounting and commerce.[32] He was an exceptionally bright student and became successful in business, banking and eventually politics. But we will see more of his story later.

How do we assess the patrol officers, particularly when one fathered and then abandoned a child? Patrol officers were given clear instructions that "Native females were off-limits. Liaisons with native females were forbidden and any breach of that rule would result in a severe reprimand, or instant dismissal."[33] Even patrol officers who received virtually no other on-the-job training were told that "sexual relations with native women were absolutely forbidden."[34]

There was good reason for this. The relationships were unequal in terms of expectations and power, and in some places, there had been

---

31. O'Neill, *Concluding Address*.
32. Callick, *Highlander with Big Shoes to Fill*.
33. Brown, *Fifty Shades of Kiap*, 12.
34. Hardy, *The DIY Cadet*, 52.

large-scale outbreaks of violence when kiaps abused their authority and "took" local women. Despite the rules, such relationships were probably common.

By all accounts, however, Brian O'Neill treated Awambo well while they were together, there was no trouble in the Wiru valley as a result of their relationship, and he eventually honored his responsibilities towards his son. Peter was fully accepted by his adoptive father's family as one of their own. Overall, Awambo and her family bore no ill will to the Australian for his behavior in their valley. The Wiru people respected Brian O'Neill, particularly because he eventually acknowledged his son and provided for him.

Brian O'Neill was followed by Alan Colton, who also married a local woman from Poloko, near Kalane. They had a son, who was named after his father. Later patrol officers were married men who came with their own families.

This was not the only district where there were children of mixed race. Many of these children were to become influential in the future of their families, their tribes, and their nation.

16

The chief goes to jail

Life in the valley was changing, and Imbinali's life was changing too.

For as long as anyone could remember, the chiefs had been the authorities in the Wiru valley and surrounding areas. They were leaders in both waging war and negotiating peace. People looked to them for wisdom and guidance, and the chiefs led the way in resolving disputes. The positions were largely hereditary, but each chief also had to demonstrate his fitness for the role. If he did not fulfil his responsibilities well, then another could take his place. The chiefs and clan leaders maintained social stability through the network of men's houses, in a system that had worked for generations.

By the mid-1960s, however, things were in flux. The white men who had arrived said there was another government now which was making new laws for the land. The patrol officers said they represented the government and were there to explain the new laws. They brought with them a team of native police officers, medical orderlies, and carriers, all from other parts of Papua New Guinea, to help enforce the new ways.

The patrol officers were trained to avoid the use of force, but from the perspective of the local people, implied threat was always present. One of the first things that patrol officers did in a new area was to demonstrate their power. They gathered the people and told them to tie a pig to a stake. Then they told everyone to stand back. Nombo and his father watched as the white man raised something called a gun. There was a loud crack and the pig fell down dead. Everyone was terrified.

The white men told them to go and look at the pig: there was a hole in its head, and a smell of burning. Clearly the white men had the power to kill. The white men were smiling as if it was all a joke, but to the local people the message was clear: obey us or we will kill you. "Peaceful penetration" was the aim, but it was accompanied by the threat of force.

The patrol officers explained they were going to build roads and schools, clinics, offices, and an airstrip. They expected the local people to participate in the work. This was in many ways good because it gave the local men an opportunity to be involved in the development of their valley. However, the practice was destructive of village life. The amount of work varied, but at times the men were expected to give "a day of work for the mission, a day for the school, a day for Council and a day for road work. Often the demands of 'development' extended these days. Little time was left for their own needs, their gardens and family affairs."[35]

Most of the tribal leaders were interested in the developments and were happy to be involved. However, there were occasions when it was impossible for the men to meet the patrol officers' demands. Despite the Australians' genuine efforts to understand local ways, they did not seem to grasp the fact that the men were already working very hard within their own villages. Both men and women spent most of their time laboring in their gardens, maintaining their villages and tending their animals. The men also spent at least two days a week hunting. They had developed this lifestyle over many centuries, maintaining complete self-sufficiency for all their food and life needs. There were also the village councils to manage and the business of overseeing the clans and tribes through exchanges and ceremonies. All this work seemed strangely invisible to the patrol officers, who assumed that their priorities should override other commitments and responsibilities.

One of the saddest days of Imbinali's life came when he arrived late for a compulsory work party. He was normally diligent in trying to cooperate with the authorities, but on this occasion, he had other commitments in his village. The policeman on duty kicked him hard on the backside and the chief fell on the ground, lying face down in the dirt in front of everyone. The policeman and the patrol officer decided to make an example of him, probably believing that if the chief disobeyed instructions, then others would also avoid work in the future. They arrested Imbinali and told him he

---

35. Weeks, *Education and Change in Pangia*, 3.

had to go to jail. They seized him together with several others and loaded them onto the back of a truck.

For Imbinali, being kicked to the ground and arrested in front of his people was a terrible humiliation. The men were then driven on a circuitous route along bumpy roads, picking up other "prisoners" at various villages, before heading towards the new jail in Pangia.

Imbinali had never been in a vehicle before and he was terribly sick. He begged his captors to let him out of the truck. At first, they refused, thinking he would run away. He promised he would not try to escape and asked if he could run beside the truck instead. They were still suspicious, but eventually they agreed to let him run beside the truck, thinking he would soon tire. However, the Australians underestimated the extraordinary fitness of the local men, and the truck had to travel slowly on the bumpy roads. Imbinali ran beside it for the rest of the two-hour journey until they arrived at the jail in Ialibu.

He was kept in prison for a month. When he came out, his tribe were glad to welcome their chief home, but no feast was held to celebrate his return. It had been a time of humiliation—a time of sorrow, not celebration.

No further harm came to Imbinali, but according to those who knew him well, something had broken in his spirit and he was never quite the same again. He had lost his own sense of dignity. He had been one of the most highly respected men in the valley and had welcomed the strangers, recognizing that change was inevitable. He had exercised his considerable authority to lead his people carefully through a difficult time of change, and in return the white men had publicly humiliated him. Imbinali realized now that the Australians had no respect for him or the system of chiefs. They had not even bothered to ask the reasons for his "misconduct" and had treated him like a naughty child.

The Australians were unaware of the effect of their actions. Imprisoning a leading man as an example to others was a long-established practice: "In prison, he learns of the wisdom and power of the white men. When he has served his time, he is in an excellent position to spread the news of the white man's law and the futility of trying to evade it."[36]

Perhaps the Australians did not fully understand the role that chiefs such as Imbinali played in maintaining order in the Highlands. Perhaps they just made a bad decision on the day. Perhaps they were simply caught up in the whole system of colonial rule, which presupposed that the

---

36. *The Cairns Daily Times.*

colonizers' perspective should prevail. The Australians had also grown up assuming that the white men knew what was best for the locals. At times they did consult with the local chiefs and leaders, but the stated purpose was to use the local authority structures as a "framework upon which to hang parallel forms of introduced lawful controls."[37] In other words, they largely valued the chiefs' authority as a tool for implementing the authority of the colonizers.

Imbinali's friends Koke Itua and Karia Wano, both sons of local chiefs, were invited to work with the Australian administration to be trained as interpreters. They were the first Wiru interpreters and were given an office and a chair for *tanim tok* (interpreting).

Years later, Koke Itua remembered: "I was so proud of that chair. They told me that when I sat on that chair, I became an Australian. It felt like such an honor. But eventually I realized that every day when I got up off that chair, I wasn't an Australian any more. I was just an Australian when it suited them. And they never gave me an Australian visa!"

Imbinali continued to support the Australian administration, as he knew there was little choice. Times had changed and there was no going back. When others wanted to react in revenge, he counselled against it and spoke of forgiveness, explaining that the white men were doing what they thought was best, they just did not understand. He advised his family and other leaders to weigh everything up and take what was good. He said to the leaders in his valley, "The white men have done more good than harm. They have stopped tribal wars and they are bringing peace. They have brought good things here like medicine and schools for our children, so we should work with them and support them."

Meanwhile, the patrol officers and police assumed that Imbinali had learned his lesson and would now be quick to obey instructions. They had no idea of the role this wise and humble man continued to play in maintaining peace and social order in the valley.

Overall, how should we judge the particular form of colonialism that was at work in Papua New Guinea? Like all human activities, it is complicated. Perhaps it is best to let Imbinali's opinion stand:

"It would have been better if they had understood more about us and our lives, but on the whole, I think they meant well."

---

37. *Circular Instruction No. 147*, 1.

17

Becoming a man

WHEN NOMBO (NOW KNOWN as Charles) was about thirteen years old, a family at Pangia Station asked him to live with them and help look after their children. This was a good arrangement as Charles was closer to his school. He was happy living there. Two years later the family decided to move to Bereina, nearer Port Moresby, and invited him to go with them so he could attend secondary school there. Imbinali and Lendepame agreed, so Charles went to Bereina.

It was a difficult time. He was lonely and homesick, and he struggled with the hot climate and strange culture. He became very ill and almost died. He eventually recovered and continued his schooling, but he was depressed and miserable and often wished he had never left his valley.

One night something changed. He began to dream again. An angel picked him up and carried him, flying through the air. Just as before, he was looking down on the land below. He began to challenge the angel, asking why life had become so hard. He had been so sick and faced so many struggles. But these were unanswerable questions, and the angel did not reply. Instead, the sense of God's presence became more and more powerful.

When he awoke, Charles felt he had been lifted up in mind, body, and spirit. His depression was completely gone.

He now began to feel that he should go to Port Moresby. So, at the age of seventeen, like many other young men, he took a boat to the capital to look for a job. Charles knew no one and stayed at the Salvation Army hostel. It was easy to find work at that time, and he was offered a job as a clerk with the Post and Telegraph Company. They organized accommodation for him and he began work immediately. He was keen to learn and completed all the training courses they offered. Then he applied for a promotion to work in the Post and Telegraph Company office in Rabaul, and he was accepted. He lived in Rabaul for three years and life was going well.

But God still had other plans. One night Charles and a friend were invited to go and watch a movie in a Rabaul park. Television and other entertainment were not available at that time, so the two young men went to see the film. Charles was captivated by a huge sign at the front: "Jesus Christ is the same yesterday, today and forever." The film was about a Christian preacher called T.L. Osborne and showed people being healed and miracles happening in other parts of the world.

Charles began to wonder: "I have been a Catholic. I've always thought that Jesus was dead, hanging on a cross. Is Jesus still alive somewhere? Is he really the same yesterday, today and forever?" His young mind began to sift what he had been taught. Was it really possible for people to do the things that Jesus did—make blind people see or lame men walk? He was deeply troubled.

Then he felt the familiar presence of the angel, just like in his dreams. It was a comforting presence he had experienced at home, then in Bereina and now in Rabaul. He heard a voice. It seemed like a rushing river, different from any voice he had heard before. The voice said, "You can do these things too."

Charles was startled, and looked around to see if someone was playing a joke on him. He was so shocked that he began to run away. But the presence of God was also very strong. As he was leaving, he heard an announcement that there would be another movie the next day.

The following day he found a bookshop and bought a Bible. He wanted to look for the words "Jesus Christ is the same yesterday, today and forever." He read the statement over and over again. He began to believe that people really could still do miracles and live like Jesus.

Then he put the Bible away. He was quite comfortable with his life and did not want religion to interrupt things. But he couldn't stop thinking about the voice saying, "You can do this too."

The next week he went to see another movie in the park. This time he arrived early and a group of people were praying. Charles heard them speaking in tongues, something he had never encountered before. He stood back, wondering what was happening. But more people gathered, and he found himself surrounded by people praying. He did not close his eyes but watched and wondered.

Then Charles felt the strong presence of the Spirit of God. It seemed to take over the whole group while they prayed. He had not experienced anything like it in any church service before.

A man announced there was a problem with the projector, so there would be no movie that night. Charles was disappointed. Then the man asked if anyone wanted to receive Jesus as savior. Charles was embarrassed and kept his head down, but he couldn't leave because he was surrounded by people. The words "Jesus Christ is the same yesterday, today and forever" kept running through his mind, and eventually he raised one finger slightly, hoping no one would see him.

Charles said to God, "If Jesus is really the same yesterday, today and forever, can you touch me?" Suddenly it was as if the power of God touched his finger. He felt a powerful presence passing through him, like a bolt of electricity running up his arm and through his body. It was wonderful, but also terrifying because he did not know what was happening.

He walked slowly out of the crowd. He didn't want to talk to anyone and he didn't want to change his life. But the presence of God was strong. He felt that all the past struggles of his life were being lifted and he was being healed and renewed.

All that night he had a sense of new life rising within him. Then at work the next day, a colleague said, "You look different. What's happened?" Charles was not sure how to respond and just said he had been to a movie. He didn't understand what had happened himself.

After work, he went straight to one of the pastors who had organized the film and told him what had happened. The pastor explained, "You asked Jesus, and He came into your life." He showed Charles passages from the Bible to help him understand Jesus and the principle of new birth.

Every evening for a month, Charles met the pastor and learned more about Jesus and the Word of God. Then he was baptized. Some of his friends came and brought a carton of beer to celebrate with him. He laughed and told them he did not drink any more. They were puzzled, but he explained his faith and they listened quietly, then said they would respect it.

Charles continued to read the Bible every day, covering the entire book from Genesis to Revelation in a few months. He also continued to attend church. There he heard people talking about being filled with the Holy Spirit, but he had never had that experience. Eventually, after three years in

Rabaul, Charles was promoted again and transferred to another job back in Port Moresby. As he was walking up the steps of the plane, he stopped at the door and turned to wave goodbye to his friends. In that moment, the Holy Spirit suddenly touched and filled him, and he began to pray silently in a language he didn't know. He found his seat on the plane, rather dazed, and sat quietly praying all the way back to Port Moresby. He felt as if he was not on the earth any more.

At Jacksons Airport, Charles got a taxi to the public servants' accommodation. While he was in the vehicle, Charles suddenly had a vision about the taxi driver.

He asked him, "Did you steal money last night?"

The taxi driver was shocked. There was a silence, and then he said, "Yes. How did you know?"

"The Holy Spirit told me."

The taxi driver was terrified. He began sweating and shaking. They talked some more, and the driver repented of his wrong doing. Charles explained Jesus to him. The driver asked Jesus to forgive him and decided to change his way of life.

From that time, Charles became involved with a charismatic church in Waigani, Port Moresby, under the leadership of a Dutch pastor called John Pasterkamp. Charles worked with YWAM (Youth with a Mission), going out on the streets in the evenings and weekends to speak to people about Jesus. In the 1970s, Port Moresby was quite safe at night—families could walk on the streets without fear. Charles got a projector, and they began to show films in parks and on the streets.

He continued to work as a public servant, but his life was shifting. John Pasterkamp became his spiritual father, mentoring Charles and teaching him about God and His Word. When Papua New Guinea gained independence in 1975, many missionaries and expatriates left, but John Pasterkamp stayed at Waigani, training many young Papua New Guinean men and women. They did a lot of outreach work, and Charles became a team leader in the city and the surrounding villages. He called his team "Life Outreach Team" and the church became known as Waigani Christian Life Centre.

Throughout this time, Charles never forgot his own village, and in 1977 he took one of his teammates back to the Wiru valley. People packed into one of the communal houses in Poloko to hear him speak about Jesus. As soon as he began talking, a young married woman started to scream. At first Charles ignored her but the screaming continued, apparently out of the woman's control.

Charles knew there was a lot of witchcraft and other spiritual activity in this village, and he sensed the crowd was turning against him and becoming potentially dangerous. He silently cried to God: "Help! I need a miracle here!"

Charles stopped preaching and looked at the young woman, who was heavily pregnant and continuing to scream. He sensed that a demonic spirit was at work, and called out in a loud voice, "In the name of Jesus, I command you to come out!"

The woman screamed again and then, to everyone's horror, lifted off the floor as if raised by an invisible hand. She fell heavily to the ground. Charles stretched out his hands, speaking in English. "Who are you?"

The lady replied in Pidgin, a language she could not normally speak, "I am her father and I am taking care of her."

Charles asked, "Who else is there?"

"No one else."

Charles commanded the spirit to leave her. The young woman sat up and looked around. The wildness was gone from her eyes and she began to cry. Others gave her water to drink as she composed herself. She said that since her father's recent death, she had felt as if something had possessed her, like a spirit of death tormenting her. Now she said it was gone and she was at peace.

The crowd's antagonism was broken. Charles began to explain who Jesus was—the God above all gods. He explained that Jesus had conquered death and there was nothing to fear from it. By the end of that day, many people in Poloko came to know Jesus.

Later Charles visited Pangia Station. There some of the local people told him about a mad woman who chased people around the village. She used to be quite normal, they said, but then suddenly changed and became disturbed. Her husband was always running after her, trying to take her home, but she was so violent that no one could get close to her.

Then Charles caught sight of her running towards him, chasing people. He waited quietly. She came near and stopped, and they stared into each other's eyes. Abruptly she jumped to one side and ran. Charles told the people to catch her and bring her back. They managed to do so and brought her to the church. Charles commanded the spirit to leave her. Immediately, her whole body relaxed and there was no more violence. Her husband was weeping as he took her home. She went on to live a normal life, having seven healthy children over the years.

These encounters with spirits were a new experience for Charles, preparing him for his work ahead.

PART 3

Opening the eyes of the blind

18

The rise of the gangs

The city of Port Moresby was growing. Large numbers of people were moving in from the villages, and this was creating new social problems. Charles began to encounter more and more men and women who had lost their way in life: they could see that the old paths would not lead them into the future, but new pathways did not yet exist in a constantly shifting world.

Displaced men no longer knew who they were or who they could trust. Charles saw their pain. In the dark hours of the night in Port Moresby, he often heard the cries of women being beaten or abused. His heart was burdened with the knowledge that this was no way for people to live.

Charles saw young men forming into gangs. In the past, these men would have been hunters and warriors, trained under the authority of the chiefs. Now the authority of the chiefs was diminished and the men's sense of identity was in tatters. They could see the wealth, luxury and comfort that white people enjoyed, but they were unable to access those things.

To the eyes of a white person, it is very easy to look at current issues of unemployment, crime, and welfare dependency in a developing country like Papua New Guinea and to assume these issues have always been there. In fact, unemployment and welfare dependency only developed after the arrival of the white man.

Back in 1912, the governor of Papua allocated a sum of money for the "maintenance and welfare of infirm or destitute natives of the territory." He was quite willing to use the money for that purpose, but he encountered an unexpected problem: "It has been impossible to find any 'destitute' natives, a fact which, I think, speaks volumes for the kindly disposition of the

Papuan natives and the care which they take of the aged and the weak. In no white man's country that I know of would a search for the 'destitute' have been in vain."[38]

As the years went on, however, the creation of a Western-style city produced an entirely new set of social dynamics. One of the tragic unintended consequences was the creation of increasingly large groups of young men, who came to the city looking for work or new opportunities but were unable to find them. Their lives had no purpose or meaning and things began to go wrong. "When community elders lose control, lifelong dreams turn to nought, meaningful employment is lost, and people experience a crisis in living. When a community experiences such a crisis, many seemingly abnormal things occur."[39]

Charles remembered the villages in the Wiru where young men were guided through life by their fathers and uncles. They all knew their place in the tribe. His father Imbinali had brought orphans into his own men's house. They lived with his tribe, eating, sleeping, and working together with the chief's own family. The *Poku* was a safe place for young boys, and young orphaned girls were welcomed into the women's houses. When the orphans were about sixteen years old, they were given help to marry or get their own house and land. There were no abandoned or homeless people in the Wiru.

Charles's heart broke for these lads in Port Moresby who were restless and without a role. The gangs they formed were a substitute for the close-knit tribes they had lost. Increasingly they turned to violence and crime.

The first gangs were groups of men from Goilala, "a district notorious for the savagery of its fighting men, from the earliest days of government contact."[40] Their ferocity towards outsiders was renowned and their district was wracked with constant tribal warfare. One of the current chiefs spoke privately about his struggles:

> In my tribe, no one has grey hair. My people keep killing each other before they are old enough to turn grey. We are a tribe of orphans, with no old people and no fathers. There is such a spirit of jealousy. If my coffee plants grow taller than yours, you will be so angry that you will come and cut my coffee down. Then I go and cut your coffee down in revenge. And so it goes on. If a man

---

38. Murray, *Papua or British New Guinea*, 35.
39. Trudgen, *Why Warriors Lie Down and Die*, 56.
40. Sinclair, *The Explorations of Ivor Champion of Papua*, 95.

builds a house that is better than his neighbor's, then the neighbor will not ask how to improve his house, he will burn the neighbor's house down. Then the neighbor burns the other man's house in revenge, so in the end, no one has a house. When people see something good, something that is better than what they have, they just want to destroy it so that no one else can have it. No one in my tribe has even finished school, because everyone hates anyone who stands taller than his brother. My people are crippled by violence and jealousy. It has been like this for generation after generation.[41]

As these groups of young men banded together, they gave themselves new group identities such as "Goipax 105" or "The G-dogs." Other gangs formed later, usually based on their members' places of origin.

At first the gang's activities were about survival and they stole in order to live. But things soon escalated. The gangs became increasingly violent, and they began to replace their long bush knives with guns. One of the gang leaders told Charles a strangely haunting story.

When he was young, this man had worked for an Australian couple as a *hausboi* (servant). He was well treated, but he could see the enormous gulf between the material wealth of his employers and the poverty of his own people, and this began to torment him. One day, after he had been drinking, he found the master's gun. He picked it up and went to find his master and mistress, then quite deliberately shot them both. Others heard the shots and came running, and found them dead.

The young killer was arrested and jailed for twenty-five years, but this did not reform him. While he was in prison, he became a hero. His story captured the imagination of other discontented young men on the streets. Many gang members began to collect guns; they bought or stole as many as they could find. Some men lay in wait near the army barracks to ambush soldiers when they came out, stealing their guns and ammunition.[42] Soon they learned how to make their own rough firearms. By the time their hero was released from jail, guns were well established in the gangs.

The man told Charles sadly, "We used to watch cowboy movies all the time. The white men made those films and showed them to us. In the movies every problem was solved with a gun. When I found my master's gun, I was being a cowboy, acting like the cowboys did in the films. No one told us those movies were fiction."

41. Private interview with a chief from the Goilala district, August 2013.
42. Private interview with former gang leader, Port Moresby, August 2013.

Part 3 | Opening the eyes of the blind

To those brought up in Western countries it may seem far-fetched that adults could watch cowboy movies and genuinely believe they present a credible pathway through life. However, indigenous people in other nations have told of similar bewilderment when they began to be bombarded with media and advertising. In Australia, people in Arnhem Land were shown government films, posters and publications informing them how to live healthy lives, and they were instructed to live according to that information. Then they started to see advertisements for products such as Coca-Cola. "We think it is good for us. We see all the healthy kids and they do all those healthy things."[43] They began to spend their limited resources on Coca-Cola for their children, thinking this was what the government was advising them to do.

No one explained to them that Coca-Cola commercials and health information were different. When advertising was explained to the people, it made no sense. Why would a government tell them things that were good and then allow someone else to tell them things that were bad?

Like the indigenous people of Arnhem Land, the young men of Papua New Guinea were brought up with tribal stories. These stories passed on the wisdom of their forefathers, giving counsel and insight into how the next generation should live. No one told to the young warriors that white men's stories were different, that they were just "entertainment" and not to be taken seriously. No one told them that movies were not expected to impart advice or wisdom about life and that the films displayed behaviors and lifestyles that should not be imitated.

The gangs became increasingly violent and armed robberies, kidnappings and carjackings became commonplace. Some parts of Port Moresby were notorious, particularly the district of Morata. Jimmy Aro, a leader of Goipax 105, was one of the gang leaders who made his base here. Soon many of the streets became no-go areas for the police. Jimmy's men would set up an ambush at a narrow bridge. When a car came, the men blocked the road, robbing the driver and sometimes stealing the car. The police were usually powerless. Even if they were called, often they could not come because gangs had stolen the wheels off the police cars or removed their engines.

Much of Morata used to be a swamp. Houses started to spring up, mostly poor shelters pieced together from bits of corrugated iron and plastic sheets. It was an ugly place, with none of the beauty or craftsmanship of the traditional villages, and people lived there because they had no choice.

---

43. Trudgen, *Why Warriors Lie Down and Die*, 134.

One young woman came to Port Moresby to find work in the 1970s. She got a job and went to live with her brother in Morata when the gangs were at their peak. Her brother was afraid for her: "Sister, this street is not good. Why did you come? It's not safe here for beautiful girls like you." She would time her run to the bus stop every morning so she got there as soon as the bus arrived. Coming home in the evening, she would get off the bus and start running: "Often men used to chase me from the bus stop and I used to run for my life. Every night I would pray, and I always locked the door as soon as I got to the house."[44]

Her fears were justified. As soon as darkness fell, the screams began from girls and women who were being raped and abused in the swamps and scrubland behind the houses in Morata. "After seven o'clock most nights I could hear girls shouting out of the swamp. They were being raped, and sometimes the men were chopping and killing them. There was nothing we could do."

When the morning light came, it was not unusual to find a girl dead or injured, left in the swampland by men whose lives were out of control.

Some women, including Jimmy Aro's wives, became involved in the gangs because of their husbands or boyfriends. But the gangs were brutal places for women. One gang leader said, "In the villages you proved you were a man by going into an enemy village and stealing one of their pigs. Now in the town we use women instead of pigs." When a young man wanted to join one of the gangs, he had to fulfil certain tasks to prove himself. Women were kidnapped and brutalized, often killed. Some women survived but found they could not go home: a few were kept captive by force or by threats, others felt too ashamed to return to their families. They became "wives" of the gangs, enmeshed in a world of violence and shame.

For Charles, the solution to this violent and destructive behavior was clear. He saw the need for jobs, decent housing and retraining for the men to help them cope with the issues of life. He was committed to addressing those needs. However, he saw another issue: "If we only attend to those needs, we are just dealing with half of the picture. There is also a problem with the spirit. We need to share the gospel with them, to deal with the problems in the spirit."

---

44. Interview, Morata, August 2013.

19

A partner for life

In the villages, it was traditional for parents to arrange marriages for their children. Charles was now living in the city, but when he went back to the village to visit his family, his father told him he should be married. His mother and father had a girl in mind and they wanted to approach her family to arrange a bride-price.

Charles was torn. He was accustomed to different ways now and did not feel attracted to this girl. However, he wanted to honor his parents and did not want to oppose them. He began to pray about the matter.

He went to see his father and explained that he wanted to honor his parents. Charles agreed to do what they asked, but suggested, "If the girl or her family do not want this, or if they refuse the bride price, can that be the end of the matter? I would like to be free then to choose my own wife."

Imbinali was pleased with Charles's reply. He was glad that his son still respected his parents and the traditional ways, so he agreed. There did not seem to be any reason why the girl's family would reject the offer of marriage with Charles.

The chief approached the girl's father and they began to negotiate a bride price. Charles, the man who worked daily with Australians in the city, found himself back in his village watching pigs being lined up and kina shells and gifts arranged as the two sides negotiated. The whole village was involved in the event. Eventually the families agreed on the bride price and the marriage was arranged.

However, soon a complication developed. One of the girl's uncles got greedy, advising her family to increase their demands. "This is a chief's son who is working in the city," he said. "Why are we satisfied with this? He can give us much more."

The girl's father listened, and even though the agreement had been settled, they went back to Imbinali to demand more pigs, more goods, and more money. For Imbinali, the decision was clear. He and Charles had agreed that if the girl's family did not stick to their agreement, then Charles was free to refuse her. Imbinali could see for himself that the girl's family was greedy and he no longer wanted an alliance with them. He told them the bride price arrangements were finished and there would be no marriage.

Charles was relieved. He had obeyed and honored his parents, but now he had a way out and was free to choose his own wife. The village girl later married someone else, so honor was restored for everyone.

Charles returned to Port Moresby and continued to preach the good news of Jesus. When he was twenty-six years old, he was praying for a wife. He felt that three things would be the sign of who the right girl was. First, she would call him on the phone. Secondly, she would love and accept him the way he was. Thirdly, she would want to serve God together with him.

Soon after he began praying like this, he went at Easter time to Popondetta, near Kokoda, with a team of evangelists. They met a group there who had organized an Easter camp for young people, with a visiting speaker from Port Moresby. One of the local leaders was a bright young woman called Lucille, who worked as the Head of Social Sciences at the local high school. She was a natural leader and offered hospitality to Charles and his team, cooking for them, and joining in their evangelism work. Charles soon felt that God was telling him this woman would be his wife. He did not know she was the firstborn daughter of the local chief.

Lucille suspected that Charles was attracted to her, but she also knew her father held strongly to the old ways. He would be reluctant to give his daughter in marriage to a man from a different tribe, especially a man from the wild Highlands! What is more, a chief's daughter, particularly a prized eldest daughter, would usually be married to the son of a chief. Lucille knew little about Charles and could not imagine her father would approve of him.

They did not know that God had also been speaking to Lucille's father. The chief had become a Christian, and a work of the Spirit of God was happening over the whole area. Lucille's father took Charles and his team around all the villages in his lands. One day Charles was washing in a river and the chief sat on a rock watching him. Much to his surprise, he heard God telling him that this young man was to marry Lucille. The chief was naturally startled: he had not experienced the Holy Spirit's voice like this before, but he had no doubt that it was the voice of God.

Meanwhile, Charles was ready to return to Port Moresby. He decided not to speak about his feelings to Lucille or her father, but prayed, "Lord, I want to be sure that this is what you want. I will not contact her; I will wait. If she is the right girl for me then let her contact me." He left his phone number and went home.

A few days later, Lucille called Charles with a story. "I'm excited! A miracle has happened. The Holy Spirit has shown me where my keys were."

Charles had been talking a lot about the Holy Spirit, telling Lucille things she had not known before. At work she held the keys for the whole Social Sciences department. One day she couldn't find the keys. She searched everywhere, without success. She went home that night worried, then she began to pray, "Holy Spirit, can you show me where the keys are?"

Immediately, she had a picture in her mind of keys hidden in a pile of papers. She went to school the next morning, saying, "If the keys are there, I will know that what I have heard about the Holy Spirit is real."

A pile of papers sat on her desk. She picked them up and the keys were underneath. From that time, she had no doubt about the power of the Holy Spirit. She called Charles and told him the story, not knowing she was fulfilling the first sign that she would be his wife.

But there was also something Charles did not know about Lucille. She too had been praying for three things in a husband: a man who loved Jesus, a man who would make Jesus the center of their home, and a man she could work with, serving God together.

Over the next few months, they continued to talk on the phone, and even though they did not meet again, both Charles and Lucille soon felt they should marry. Charles explained his feelings to her but also said he had a strong calling from God on his life. He told Lucille about his desire to reach the lost in Port Moresby and said he could not marry anyone who was not willing to partner in his work. Lucille had come to love Charles, and she also had a strong love for God. She was committed to serving Him and was deeply satisfied at finding a man who shared her longings.

Lucille was afraid to tell her father since she and Charles were not following the old rules. Women did not choose their own husbands, especially a man from a different tribe and district. Her father was coming to visit her in Popondetta, and she prayed for courage to talk to him.

"Do you remember a young man who was here?"

He interrupted her. "You don't need to tell me." He described the moment on the riverbank when God had told him Charles would marry his daughter. Lucille was amazed and delighted.

The chief had his turn to be amazed and delighted when he discovered that Charles was an educated man with a good job and the son of a great chief. Lucille's father could not have found a more suitable match for his bright, educated eldest daughter.

They met in April 1978, got engaged in September and were married in December. Lucille got a job teaching in Port Moresby, and then in 1980 both she and Charles spent a year in full-time study at Life Bible College. In 1981 they returned to their jobs in telecommunications and teaching.

Charles continued his preaching and his street work among the growing number of gang members in Port Moresby. Every week, young men and women from the gangs came to their home for meals, barbeques, and Bible studies. Their house became a haven for many of these troubled young people as Charles, Lucille and the Life Outreach Team worked with them, building relationships, and gaining their trust.

20

Gangs, sorcery, and men who can't smile

In the educated West people are cynical about spiritual explanations for human problems. But most people in Papua New Guinea have no doubt that spirituality is real. The spirit world has always been right there at the forefront of their daily lives, so whenever there is a problem, it cannot be fully resolved without attending to the needs of the spirit.

Gang members often told Charles about witchcraft and sorcery in the gangs. These were common in tribal culture throughout Papua New Guinea: "Our tribes are in the grip of sorcery. The chiefs in my area are expected to be chief sorcerers, skilled in witchcraft and magic. They talk with spirits and they use spirits' power. We will never be able to progress until we leave witchcraft and sorcery behind."[45]

The young gang members grew up in villages where witchdoctors, sorcerers and *glasmen* (seers) had power. They brought that culture to the city where they encountered new varieties of spirituality. Sadly, some early gang leaders latched onto elements of white man's religions in a way that was distorted and destructive.

The gangs developed their own identities, often based on animals. Many tribes had animals as totems, but in tribal culture this was usually perceived in a positive light. Charles's tribe, for example, had the cassowary as their totem because it was tall and fast-running, strong, and upright like a man. The gangs began to adopt the identity of animals which were seen as less

---

45. Interview with a chief from the Goilala district, August 2013.

admirable, such as rats or dogs (for example the "G-dogs" or "Goilala dogs"). The animal identity somehow seemed to further degrade their humanity.[46]

Some gangs developed rituals which blended the worst of tribal witchcraft with borrowings from Satanism. This involved brutalization, kidnapping, rape and killing, even culminating in the eating of the victim's flesh, or drinking their blood. There were gang leaders who spoke openly with Lucifer and called on his powers. "Our leader would walk up to a locked door. He would put his hands on the lock—even a big, strong lock—and speak to the lock in the name of Lucifer. The lock would break open in his hands. Yes, I saw that with my own eyes."[47]

Port Moresby was becoming a very troubled city. It was a strange, confusing world for young men, and many became increasingly lost and angry. They became known as "raskols." In English this word sounds like naughty children, but the raskols became hardened criminals, committing carjackings, kidnappings, armed robbery, and murder.

As well as doing his street work, Charles began to speak more publicly. In 1982 he and Lucille established a church in Morata. Then he and his team decided to hold a rally in the grounds of the University of Papua New Guinea. Charles was driven by a verse from the Bible: "My heart's desire is that they may be saved."[48] In his mind, the words were "My heart's desire is that Papua New Guinea may be saved."

Hundreds of people came to hear him preach. He spoke about a loving God who wanted all people to have life to the full. He explained the need for repentance, turning away from the past, and talked about Jesus as the answer to the future.

Preaching, prayer, confession and repentance are not exactly popular words in First World societies, and people there are likely to react to them with laughter. But when Charles preached in Port Moresby, many people responded with tears, asking God for forgiveness, and giving their lives to Jesus.

The following year, 1983, Charles organized another rally at a sportsground in the suburb of Hohola, holding meetings every night for a week.

---

46. The sister of a gang member in Australia told me a similar story about gangs in Melbourne. Gang members often take on the identity of an animal such as a rat. Many of the gang's customs and rituals are then based around that animal identity. For example, the trademark of one gang was cutting off the little finger of a victim; they called this "cutting off the rat's tail." Private conversation, Melbourne, 2012.

47. Interview with former gang member, Port Moresby, July 2012.

48. Adapted from Romans 10:1.

Part 3 | Opening the Eyes of the Blind

Hundreds came. During that week, Charles was at Ela Beach one afternoon. He noticed a man wearing a T-shirt saying "Full Gospel Businessmen's Fellowship" and stopped to speak to him.

Dale Fenton and his wife, Betty, were Americans on holiday. Dale had fought in Papua New Guinea during World War 2, and all his life he had talked to his family about that country, often crying as he remembered the place and the people. His wife decided that when he turned sixty, she would surprise him with tickets to Papua New Guinea, so here they were.

They talked for a long time with Charles and that night came to the rally. They were deeply moved by the presence of God and by seeing people healed and lives changed. When they returned to the USA, they wrote to Charles and said they wanted to "adopt" him as part of their family. They have continued to be close friends over the years.

THROUGHOUT THE EARLY 1980S, the outreach teams went onto the streets at night. As darkness fell, they set up an outdoor projector and showed movies such as the *Jesus* film or *The Cross and the Switchblade*, which told the story of the New York gang leader Nicky Cruz.

Nicky's early life in Puerto Rico was steeped in fear: "Mama worked with Papa as a medium. Our house was the headquarters for all sorts of voodoo, séances, and sorcery. My early childhood was filled with fear. I was afraid of the sorcery that took place each night."[49] He ran away from home but carried the fear and anger with him to the streets of New York, where he became involved with gangs at an early age. Later he had an encounter with God and turned from his life of violence.

Crowds gathered to watch each night, and when the film was over, families, women and children went home. But some of the men lingered. Charles found that the ones who stayed were often raskols who wanted to talk about what they had seen. Danger was always present, and Charles never worked without a team of mature people positioned around the area to pray.

Sometimes men would get argumentative and aggressive, but Charles was not easily intimidated. More than once a man pointed a gun at him and ordered him to leave. He refused to go. One gang leader produced a gun and told Charles, "You go away or I'll kill you."

Charles felt the power and presence of the Spirit of God on him. Instead of backing off, he stepped towards the raskol.

"I'm not leaving. You go away."

---

49. Cruz, *Run Baby Run*, 4–5.

The man took a step back, but shouted again, "Leave now or I'll kill you!"

Again, Charles stepped forward. "No, I'm not going to leave. You are the one who must leave."

Once again, the raskol stepped back. And so the contest continued: each time the threat was made, Charles stepped forward and the man retreated. Eventually he turned and ran.

Many of the crowd had disappeared, fearing murder, but some came out from their hiding places when the danger was past. Charles began to tell them about the power of a living God.

Charles began to realize that many of the gang members were afraid of him. He asked one man, "Why are you so frightened?"

The man shifted his feet, unable to look Charles in the face. "I'm scared of you. Your eyes are like a torch. It's like you are seeing everything in me."

When Charles told the raskols about the possibility of a new life in Jesus, he pressed them hard. If a man showed interest and wanted to be saved from his life of fear and pain, Charles would ask him to raise his hands publicly, in front of other gang members. He told them they could receive Jesus, the Son of God, who was sent by the Father to bring life and light into the world. The old would be gone and they would become clean and new.

Charles knew that any man who wanted to change his life would have a hard road ahead, so he had to be clear about his decision. It was a hard but powerful message, and many heard it and believed.

By 1984, many raskols had given their lives to Jesus, but they were finding life difficult. They could not go back to the gangs, but most had no job or decent place to live, so it was virtually impossible for them to make progress. Charles knew there was a risk of them returning to their old lives. He prayed about what to do.

Meanwhile, a man called Dr James Ferguson, director of the counselling agency Lifeline in Papua New Guinea, was concerned about the same problem. He offered to donate funds so that Charles could build a dormitory for the men.

They found land in Morata and, under the direction of a German volunteer, began to build a dormitory. Dr Ferguson got hold of concrete building blocks, leftovers from the construction of the National Parliament building, and some of the former raskols provided labor. At the beginning there were no toilets or kitchen, so the men dug a pit toilet and cooked over fires.

Soon after, Charles and Lucille decided to move onto the Morata property. A group called Pacific Islands Ministry (PIM) built a house for them, and they moved there in 1985. Their daughter, Merlinda, was four years old and their son, Enoch, three. The founder of PIM, Neil Kooyers, became a strong supporter of their work, and offered financial support so Charles could leave his job as a public servant and work full-time among the gangs.

So, Charles and Lucille lived and worked on-site, bringing up their young children among ex-criminals, murderers, and rapists. Later they said it never occurred to them to be worried about living surrounded by ex-gangsters. Their house was always a safe place for their children, and Enoch particularly spent every possible minute outside with the young men. They had four acres of land, and the Papua New Guinea defense forces offered to clear and level the rough ground, dig drains, and build roads.

They called the place the "Jesus Centre" because they wanted Jesus to be the center of everything that they did.

WHEN MEN CAME TO the Jesus Centre, recovery took a long time. First the team helped them come to terms with their past. This was a painful process as their lives had often been horrific. Charles discovered that the young men he had met on the streets at night had sometimes come straight from killings, rapes, or perverse rituals. Even knowing these things, Charles still could not see these men as dangerous—he was somehow blind to the full horror of what was happening around him. He only felt what he calls "the anointing of God."

Charles began to realize that the men in the gangs never smiled because they were carrying so much pain. They were often brutalized to the point of thinking that beatings, violence, and bloodshed were normal life. They had learned never to show weakness or softness and were immersed in a world of fear.

When they came to the center, the violent practices stopped but the fear and pain were still there. The men had lost their humanity and their human identity, even giving up their own names. They were given new names in the gangs—sometimes a man might be known by as many as ten nicknames, and these became his new identities. When a man left a gang, reopening his own identity was a painful business because it meant opening himself again to emotions. Sometimes it was months before a man could bring himself to reveal his own name.

Often it took half a year before he began to smile. When a man was able to smile again, it meant life was returning.

21

Even the birds disappeared

> "How long will the land mourn and the grass of every field wither? Because of the evil of its residents, animals and birds have been swept away."
>
> JEREMIAH 12:4

BY THE 1980S THERE were probably about four thousand men involved in gangs around Papua New Guinea. Gang activities were headline news. Fierce competition existed between the rival groups: if one gang made the headlines one week, another gang would try to outdo them the following week. It was a campaign of terror, and Morata seemed to be the worst place of all.

Local people have a strange memory of that period. They say, "Even the birds disappeared." This was probably partly natural: as more people lived around Morata, trees were cut down and bushland disappeared. Boys used slingshots to kill birds for fun or food. Many of the older people, however, felt there was more to it than that. To them it was a sign that something was deeply wrong and the whole balance of nature was fundamentally damaged. Whatever the reason, Morata was not a good place to be.

Charles began to befriend three gang leaders in the Morata area: Jimmy Aro and Simon John, who both led groups of Goipax 105, and Kakana, who led Bomai 58. Goipax and Bomai were the biggest gangs, with different groups across the country. Simon John was a small man, but he was the son of a powerful chief and held strong influence over his own gang members as well as among other gang leaders. Charles prayed for these men and spent time getting to know them.

Part 3 | Opening the Eyes of the Blind

One morning Charles and Lucille got their children ready for school as usual. When he opened the door of his pick-up truck to climb in, something did not seem right. He realized the windscreen was gone—someone had stolen it. He took the children to school on the bus and prayed all the way home. In his mind he saw a picture of a street nearby and, as if in a movie, an image of two men with his windscreen. When he got home, he called two friends and they drove together down the street he had "seen."

They found the place and two men were standing in front of a house. As soon as they saw Charles they started to run. Charles walked towards the house and saw his windscreen. The two men were watching, from a distance.

"I'm going to take my windscreen now," Charles called out.

"It's ours. We bought it," they shouted back.

"If you bought it then show me a receipt. I'm going to take it now. If you bring me a receipt then I will give it back to you."

He picked up the windscreen and put it in the pick-up. The men did not move. They never showed up with a receipt, and word got around that if you stole from Charles, he would come and find you.

Charles wanted to find the best possible model for rehabilitation programs. He looked at programs run by various organizations and continued to pray and ask questions. In 1986 the family received an unexpected letter from their adopted American parents, the Fentons, who offered to buy tickets for Charles, Lucille, Merlinda, Enoch, and one-year-old Betty to visit them in Ohio. They accepted the offer with delight. Charles felt it was an answer to prayer because he wanted to visit Teen Challenge's rehabilitation center in Los Angeles, established by Nicky Cruz, the former leader of the Mau-Mau gang in New York.

They had a wonderful time with the Fentons and were able to get to Los Angeles. Staff at the Teen Challenge center made them welcome and showed them around. Charles liked what he saw, especially the focus on the whole person: human beings are mind, body and spirit, and the needs of all those aspects must be addressed. He decided that this was the best model for the Jesus Centre too.

By this time his work was attracting attention in Papua New Guinea and among expatriates from around the world. Many groups and organizations contributed funds, expertise, and resources. The Corrective Institutions Commissioner in Port Moresby approached Charles, saying he would like to send men on parole and men newly released from prison to the Jesus

Centre. Like the raskols, men who came out of prison found it difficult to adjust to normal life. Over time the Jesus Centre also became known as the "Halfway House," providing a halfway point between prison and normal society. Charles and Lucille privately thought of it as "halfway between earth and heaven." Others would not have described Morata as heavenly—it was still a dangerous place to live.

One night, some men from Goipax 105 hijacked a car in Morata and Charles happened to see them on the road near his home. He stepped out into the narrow street and held up his hand, calling for them to stop. One leaned out of the window, shouting at him to get out of the way. He called again, "Stop!" They accelerated towards him.

Charles saw the car speeding straight at him and then suddenly everything went blank. He came to and found himself standing in the middle of the road. He turned and looked behind him. He could see the car disappearing along the dusty road. He went home, feeling a little bewildered and wondering what had happened.

Next morning, the group of men came to the church. The leader went inside and saw Charles preaching. He came out, his face shocked and his eyes staring, and the whole group fled in terror. Later they returned to talk to Charles. The men all said that Charles had not moved from the middle of the road and they had run him down. There was no way anyone could have survived, and they were astonished to see him alive.

What happened? Charles does not know, but he had no pain and not a mark on his body.

The men who tried to kill Charles said they now knew he was a man of God and they wanted to change. Some joined the Halfway House and committed their lives to God.

22

Public floggings?

In 1984 crime seemed to be skyrocketing all over the country. On 16 October 1984 the National Cabinet met to discuss the rise in lawlessness, including armed robberies and pack rapes. After the gang rape of a nine-year-old girl and two women, all New Zealanders, a crowd of about twenty-five thousand people marched to the government offices to protest about the law-and-order situation. Some even called for public flogging and hanging for the rapists.

Charles firmly believed that floggings and tougher punishments were not the answer. He longed to see a real change in the culture of Port Moresby and other cities in Papua New Guinea. He wrote at the time:

> Law and order has been a very emotional issue this year in Port Moresby and other centers. Pack rape, breaking and entering, and armed hold-ups have been given wide exposure in the media. Calls have been made to re-introduce the death penalty as well as to allow public flogging. The Government has now come up with some tough measures to punish and deal with crime offenders. Will all these tough measures heal society? What is the answer to our increasing problem of crime?[50]

Charles believed that the solution was to address the needs of the spirit, soul, and body, and he continued to declare that Jesus was the answer. He did not say this lightly: his claim was born of years of experience in seeing

---

50. Lapa, *Operation Tanim Bel*, 2.

men's lives permanently turned around. "Unless a person is changed within, born again spiritually, the problems are there to stay," he said.[51]

Time after time, he had seen this "change from within." John was one of Port Moresby's most wanted criminals and gang leaders with a history of armed robbery and murder. One day John's life completely changed. Later he spoke out about crime and the solutions:

> The Government would be wasting time, money, and manpower in measures that in the long term would not solve crime. Criminals move when faced with and placed under difficult circumstances. There is no reason for the introduction of capital punishment, public flogging and hanging. Criminals are human beings and should be treated as such. I got converted.[52]

Story after story confirmed Charles's experiences. Tom, a leader of the Morata Boys, left school because his family could not afford to pay the fees. He searched for work but could not find a job. Eventually he became frustrated and set up the Bomai 007 gang, based in Morata. They stole to survive, breaking into houses and holding up vehicles.

One night he was walking past a tiny church and something made him stop. Lucille saw him and invited him in. Charles was preaching. "Every word that was spoken was saying something to me," he said later. "For the rest of that meeting I was in tears." Tom made a decision that night to change: "I believe I have found the real thing in Jesus." He said that when he was living in crime, he had never felt he was a "real Papua New Guinea citizen, but now I am a recognized citizen because I am somebody in Jesus."[53]

The gangs had given Tom an identity, but it was with a diminished sense of self. It was only when he was changed from within that he felt he was fully human.

Henry formed a gang called the Black Vavas [brothers] which grew to over 300 men, including his younger brother James. They committed robberies, carjackings and rape. Yet in June 1983, Henry suddenly disbanded the gang. What happened?

First, James heard Charles speaking about Jesus and decided to find out more about God and His love. James went back to Henry and told him, "We have really found the light." Henry did not believe what James was

---

51. Lapa, *Operation Tanim Bel*, p. 3.
52. Peng, *Convert Criminals to Christianity*.
53. *Niugini Nius*, 26 April 1985, 25–26.

saying but went to see for himself. Both decided to convert to Christianity, and they disbanded the gang. It was that simple.

"I can say that Jesus Christ is the only answer to the problems we have today." That is Henry's belief, and his own life is the living proof. He began to make furniture for Lifeline and stayed free of crime.

Many hundreds in the gangs saw transformed lives like these.

Wane was not like his fellow gang members because he did not steal to survive. His father was reasonably well off and Wane had everything he needed. But he was bored and looking for excitement, so he joined a gang for fun. Soon he found himself immersed in crime and his life began to go downhill. One day he was invited to hear Charles preach and on the spur of the moment he went. He heard the message of God's love for him, and decided to leave he left the gang, saying, "Jesus changed me."

Roy was in serious trouble. He had broken into houses and stolen vehicles. The police caught him and beat him, trying to force him to confess and tell them about his gang. But he would not speak: "There was an understanding with all gang members that you do not breathe a word, whatever the police do to you." He was trapped in a cycle of crime with no way forward. He hated everyone and trusted nobody. But Roy too found that Jesus was the answer to his misery: "Now I have peace, and I can say I love the people I see around me. In the past I hated everyone and there was no peace in me."[54]

Converting to Christianity did not mean the raskols' crimes disappeared, but all these men were ready to face up to what they had done. For some this meant going to the police to confess. One former gang leader even made a public declaration in the national *Niugini Nius* newspaper: "On behalf of my members I would like to say how sorry we are to the police, the government and the members of the public for our actions in the past."[55]

Some men began new lives, working or learning a new trade. Others went to jail. Michael spoke from prison where he was serving time for robbery, breaking and entering, and two charges of escaping from prison: "Very often I ended up in police stations. They used to beat me up, drag me, treat me very badly, and say to me you rascal, criminal, you are a dirty creature." Like so many others, Michael believed that was who he was. After he decided to become a follower of Jesus, he found a new identity: "But the Lord Jesus loved the poor like you and me. I am now a changed person, and set free by our Lord Jesus. In my outward appearance I am not

---

54. *Niugini Nius*, p. 26.
55. *Niugini Nius*, p. 26.

free. But in my inner spirit I am set free by our Lord Jesus. I know that I am in prison but my spirit is not in chains or prison."[56]

Neither jail nor heavy punishments caused inner change. Charles continued to maintain that prison, public floggings and even the threat of the death penalty could not really help these men. What he witnessed, time after time, was a deep internal transformation in young raskols' lives, brought about by an encounter with God's unconditional love.

---

56. *Operation Tanim Bel: Arawa Crusade*, p. 7.

23

Converting the white heathens

ALTHOUGH PAPUA NEW GUINEA in the 1980s was perceived as a dangerous place for white people, many "expats" from all around the world continued to make it their home.

Bob Browne grew up in London. He went to the local Anglican church with his parents, but by the time he was about sixteen church seemed meaningless, so he stopped going. He was a gifted artist and trained in art and design. In his twenties, he travelled to Morocco and was profoundly affected by the poverty he saw there. Later he went to Papua New Guinea with a volunteer organization and ended up staying for the rest of his life. He married a local journalist and became the most famous cartoonist in the Pacific.

Bob was always interested in social justice, but had lost his early faith. "I became a successful man with a well-paid job, big house, a lovely wife, two cars—anything a man could want. And I achieved it on my own effort." But something occurred over which he had no control. "Then my wife gave birth to a baby boy, but he became very sick. And no matter what I tried, there was nothing that I could do to help him. I found myself one night crying out to God to help me."[57] Tragically, the baby died.

For more than a year, Bob struggled with life, sensing that God was there but feeling unworthy and not good enough for Him. One day a priest from Brisbane visited him and told him that it was simple: "Jesus died for you. God loves you anyway—no matter how hard you try, Jesus has already paid the price." Suddenly Bob seemed to understand and decided to begin

---

57. *Operation Tanim Bel*, p. 4.

a new life with Jesus. "God did not save my son, who died when he was four weeks old. But he saved me."

Bob had come to help the people of Papua New Guinea, but instead he gained something: he found faith instead of cynicism. He decided to become a pastor and preacher: "Healings, miracles, all these things I now know through having given my life to Christ." He and Charles became close friends, and Bob used his cartoon skills to help Charles in his work.

CHARLES WAS ALWAYS KEEN to learn, and in 1986 he had the opportunity to attend a world evangelism conference in Amsterdam, led by the renowned American evangelist Billy Graham. Charles led a group of about seventy Papua New Guinean evangelists. They loved the inspirational teaching and returned home energized, freshly inspired to take the message of Jesus to their people. Charles continued to preach to large crowds across the country, from the cities to the villages.

MEANWHILE, BACK IN THE Wiru valley, Charles's sister Takuame had been busy in her village. Since taking up her role as peace child, she had settled happily into Chief Yapera's tribe. Like the rest of his tribe, she had adopted the Christian faith.

They had a new cause for excitement in their village when an American anthropologist called Sally Bruce Seddon arrived and asked if she could stay with them. She told them she wanted to study the role of women in their society. They were intrigued and rather puzzled about what this stranger really wanted, but they welcomed her with good will.

Sally began to learn the Wiru language and Takuame became one of several informants for her anthropological work. Sally became a close friend of Takuame, Yapera and their family.

One thing surprised and saddened Takuame, however: this young American did not seem to know Jesus. Takuame and others had a strong faith and often prayed for their friend. They spoke to Sally about their faith, but it meant little to her at the time though she loved them dearly.

Sally's time in the village came to an end, and on her last day she was sitting with Yapera in the compound that had been her home. Yapera had been a grandfather to her. He had accompanied her on field trips, protected her comings and goings, and now, seeing how troubled she was at the prospect of leaving the next day, Yapera began to speak to her searching heart.

Sally said later, "His words brought solace. Even though I did not understand the Christian life, I felt as though all the miracles here were something I would never experience again. I actually wondered if I was leaving the God of the universe here on this small mountaintop."

Later that afternoon, Yapera, Koke, his wife Kanoli and their son Uria, all gathered around Sally and began to pray for her journey back to America. One of them prayed, "Lord, let Sally sit next to a young Christian girl on the plane. Lord, let this young lady be a daughter of missionaries, and let them talk about Jesus all the way to Hawaii."

Sally tells the story:

> I was shocked to hear them pray with such stunning specificity but said nothing. The next day they all met me at the airport and we bade tearful goodbyes. I went up to the desk and the lady behind the counter asked me where I would like to sit. I looked up, expecting a number to just drop from heaven the way it would in the village, but I didn't hear or see anything. After an awkward silence I asked to be seated anywhere in the non-smoking section of the plane. The computer spat out a boarding pass and seat allocation.
>
> People were already boarding. I took my seat and looked anxiously around.... There was a sea of empty seats all around me. Just before the doors shut, a young lady jumped on board. I studied her closely as she looked at her boarding pass and navigated her way towards my section. She stood in the aisle next to me, verified her seat and sat down beside me! My heart was thundering in my chest. The words that the family had prayed were running through my head. I broke the silence and cut to the chase.
>
> "Hi, who are you?"
>
> "Who am I? I live here. My parents are missionaries."
>
> "WHAT??? Are you—could you be a *Christian?*"
>
> "Yes!" She was a little started at my piercing questions.
>
> "And how about you?" she asked. "Are you a Christian?"
>
> "I . . . I do not know," I stammered. I could barely breathe. The presence of Jesus and the Holy Spirit was so overwhelming. Then, *exactly* according to the Word of the Lord spoken through Yapera and the family, we talked about Jesus all the way to Hawaii."[58]

Things had come full circle. American Christians had once come to the Wiru valley to convert the "heathens," and now, just twenty years later, the Wiru people were converting Americans.

Several years after Sally completed her project in the Wiru valley, she moved to Port Moresby and worked for the government. She married a local man and had two daughters. Sally became a one of Charles's strong

---

58. Sally Hill, private letters, 2015.

supporters, writing publicity materials for the evangelism crusades and producing a magazine about the work. Later her husband died. Sally and her beautiful adult daughters now live in the USA.

Many nations that used to send missionaries are now increasingly secular, and in the developed world there is much public cynicism about Christianity. The Christian world has shifted: a faith that used to be based in Europe is now stronger elsewhere, with believers in Africa, Asia and South America far outnumbering those in Europe, America, or Australia. It is not uncommon for non-believers to travel to a developing country and find themselves in a spiritual crisis, or rather, a "crisis of cynicism" as they encounter people of faith perhaps for the first time in their lives.

The story of Jesus works in any time, place, or culture.

24

When gang rape happens, where is God?

ONE MORNING, A MESSENGER came to Charles and Lucille at the Halfway House. A thirteen-year-old girl had gone missing, and her parents were beside themselves. They thought she might have been kidnapped by a gang.

Charles and Lucille called Simon John, the former gang leader who now worked for them, and asked if he could do anything. Simon knew that a gang leader had been released from prison the previous day. Usually when that happened, the gang would kidnap a young girl to give to their leader. Simon knew that the other gang members would not talk, so he decided to go and see the man himself. In the past they had been close friends.

Lucille went to the parents and found their whole family gathered, crying and mourning. She told them there was a possible lead and urged them to pray. She left them praying and returned home.

Simon drove to where the gang leader was likely to be, praying hard all the way. The man greeted him enthusiastically.

"Hey, how are you? What can I do for you? Do you want anything? Anything you want, I'll give it to you." He seemed on top of the world.

Simon spoke quietly. "A girl is missing. Do you know anything about her?"

To his surprise, the man replied, "You are lucky. She's here."

Simon said he wanted to take her home. The gang leader had promised to give Simon anything he wanted, so he agreed. "You are lucky, my friend," he said again. "We were just waiting for a car to arrive so we could take her up to the mountains and kill her."

He took Simon to another room. The girl was lying there, barely conscious. Simon carried her to his car and drove her back to the Halfway House. When he got there, he called Lucille from the car and the two of them managed to get the girl inside without attracting attention. She was in deep shock and still barely conscious. Lucille sobbed as she cleaned her up and put clean clothes on her. When the parents arrived, she told them to take the girl straight to hospital.

The parents never came back to thank Simon for saving their daughter's life. Maybe the memories were too painful.

Through the 1980s many girls were abducted and killed by the gangs, but some survived and stayed with their captors. It was difficult for them to leave because they carried so much trauma and shame. In order to survive, they had to put aside virtually all human feelings and become emotionally dead. When they walked away from that nightmare world, it was not easy to recover.

In 1992 Charles and Lucille built a women's dormitory at the Halfway House, with funds donated by the Steamships Trading Company. The women's rooms were prepared and the kitchen and bathroom facilities were in place.

Charles and Lucille now had four young children: Merlinda, Enoch, Betty, and Pamela. One evening, just before the women's dormitory was due to open, Merlinda and Betty were in the new building with a young woman called Enjo, helping her to bake cakes. They asked Lucille if they could all stay in the new dormitory overnight. Lucille agreed, so Merlinda (aged about ten) and Betty (aged about six) settled down to sleep in one of the rooms with Enjo. Charles and Lucille were nearby in their own house on the property.

They were all fast asleep until Betty suddenly woke up in the middle of the night. She opened her eyes. In the moonlight she could see a man's arm, reaching round the bedroom door. She held her breath as she watched the door open. A small man crept into the room. Betty could see many other men crowding behind him in the corridor. She shrank back under the blanket, not daring to move.

Enjo woke up. She did not scream or shout, but began to speak to the man slowly and calmly. Betty heard Enjo saying, "Please don't hurt the little girls. Just please don't hurt the little girls." Betty did not know what she meant.

By now Merlinda was wide awake and realized what was happening. She sat up and pulled her sister, still wrapped in the blanket, towards her, cradling her between her knees. Merlinda covered them both with the blanket, wrapping her arms around Betty and shielding her ears. She whispered, "Close your eyes, stay still and be very quiet. Don't be afraid."

The short man came towards them, then hesitated and turned back to Enjo. Betty was terrified. Merlinda continued to reassure her, "We'll be alright. Don't be afraid."

As the sisters sat curled up together, the men formed a line from inside the room out into the corridor. One of the men recognized the two young girls. He had been at the Halfway House but had gone back to the gangs. For a moment he was frozen with fear, unsure what to do. Then he gathered himself and realized he had to get the girls out of the room. He lowered his voice and as discreetly as possible told them to follow him into the adjoining bathroom. He told them to lock the door, hide and stay quiet.

Meanwhile, back in the bedroom, Enjo recognized the small man. He had also been at the Halfway House before running away to rejoin the gangs. He and other gang members knew about the new house for girls and had come to cause trouble. One man after another raped Enjo throughout the night.

In the early hours of the morning the men left and Enjo ran for help. She didn't know where the two girls were. Everyone looked for them, calling their names, but they were still hiding, too scared to move or reply. Charles and Lucille feared the gang had taken them. Many people searched the creek and swampy bushland surrounding the property, not knowing if they were dead or alive.

Eventually, as the sun was coming up, Merlinda realized she could hear the voice of Uncle Zan, the Halfway House manager. She and Betty came out of hiding and ran to him. Uncle Zan shouted for joy. Tears streamed down his face as he carried the girls to their house. For Charles and Lucille, it was an unforgettable moment. They were profoundly grateful to Enjo, whose first thought had been to plead for Merlinda and Betty's safety.

Strangely, years later Merlinda and Betty said that even after this experience they were not scared about staying on the property. They couldn't explain why—somehow, they just knew they would be all right. It was still their home; their family was there and they felt safe.

And what of Enjo? She was of course deeply shocked and in need of care. However, her faith in God was strong. She continued to serve God and went on to lead a happy and healthy life.

It is not easy to understand such events. How can God allow them to happen? God is always a loving Father. No father would want his daughter to endure such an experience—God is always good. The men who attack girls are doing wrong. God has no part in such evil, but God can restore, heal, and redeem. Enjo eventually forgave the men. She found peace and contentment despite the harm done to her, and she used her experiences to help others.

God was not in the abuse, but He was certainly there in the healing, forgiveness, and redemption. The men and women of the Halfway House learn a foundational truth. They shout it loudly and often: *God gutpela olgeta taim! Olgeta taim, God is gutpela!* God is good all the time! All the time, God is good!

God is good all the time. When we are treated badly, it is not from God. God is not an abuser and His hands are not cruel. God is good, He is love and He is life.

25

What we need is tanim bel

WITH THE CHURCH IN Morata thriving and the Halfway House continuing to grow, from the mid-1980s to the early 1990s Charles took teams across the nation to run "crusades" in different cities. They called these crusades "Operation Tanim Bel," *tanim bel* meaning "a turning or change of heart" in Tok Pisin.

The approach was the same in each place. First Charles would approach the leaders of all the Christian churches in a town and outline his plans. He remembered clearly the inter-church rivalries of early missionary days and was keen to see churches working in harmony.

Next, they would set up a leadership team with representatives from all the churches. The team's job was to prepare for the campaign through prayer and make all the practical arrangements. Charles gathered enormous support from musicians, business people, community leaders and politicians as well as churches. The men from the Halfway House were always involved, helping with the work, telling their stories, and counselling other young men with similar experiences.

Thousands came to the crusades and the stories were extraordinary.

IN 1986, IN KIMBE on the island of West New Britain, a young blind girl came and people prayed for her. Suddenly she could see. A man involved in sorcery, witchcraft and black magic came forward saying he did not want to practice those things anymore and handed over his basket of fetishes to be burned.[59]

---

59. *Operation Tanim Bel: Kimbe Crusade*, 1.

While he was preaching, Charles often felt that God was giving him words for a particular person. One night in Kimbe, he publicly challenged a gang leader in the crowd. He told the man to accept Jesus and warned him that his life was going to be in danger the following day. The man chose to ignore the words and walked away. The next day he tried to rob a truck, but one of his victims fought back with a machete. The gang leader was struck on the neck and killed.[60]

The story spread rapidly and even more people came to hear Charles preach, believing that the power of God was on him.

Another man who came to the Kimbe crusade was called Daniel. He was known as a drunkard and street fighter in his home town, and he beat his wife, Lynn, virtually every day. She described him as a "beast": "He would belt me up for no reason and I was covered with bruises and in pain. He would chase me out of the house with a knife or an axe, threatening to cut us with them. One night he heated an iron hammer on the stove and tried to put it on my face."

Lynn began to pray with some friends and eventually Daniel surrendered his life to God. In his own words, "The Lord restored me." Or as Lynn put it, "After five solid years of complete suffering, pain, and difficulties, the Lord God Almighty completely changed my husband. Now I see real joy, peace, and love in our home."[61]

Another extraordinary moment came in Goroka in 1987, when Charles called for anyone who needed healing to come forward. Some people carried in a young boy called Robin. Robin had been paralyzed from the waist down since a car accident ten years earlier, and since then he had been lying in the Goroka hospital. When he was prayed for that day, he suddenly got to his feet and began to walk, then run and jump around. His excitement was unstoppable. He began to shout, praising God.

The effect on the crowd was electric. One of Robin's relatives, who had been caring for him in hospital, was so amazed that he began to cry and committed his life to Jesus on the spot. A Catholic priest also came forward for prayer, saying he had never seen a miracle like that before.[62]

A God who can make the blind to see and the lame to walk? Charles was simply following in the footsteps of his Master Jesus, "the same yesterday, today and forever."

60. *Operation Tanim Bel: Kimbe Crusade*, 5.
61. *Operation Tanim Bel: Kimbe Crusade*, 10–11.
62. *Operation Tanim Bel: Goroka Crusade*, 6.

Part 3 | Opening the Eyes of the Blind

In Rabaul in 1988, the news was running stories about a young rapist who was on the run. Sixteen-year-old Francis had been convicted of raping a young mother and sentenced to nine years in prison. Minutes later he escaped from custody. While Charles was preaching, this young lad crept into the crowd. He listened to the story of God's love and felt his heart pounding. Then one ex-raskol after another got up to tell how he used to live in constant fear of being arrested, but now Jesus had changed his life. The young escapee began to cry.

Charles invited anyone who wanted to know Jesus to come to the front. Francis got up immediately and went forward. He told Charles who he was and said he wanted to repent.

The local police commander, John ToGuata, was also in the crowd. He was called and the young escapee handed himself in, saying he was willing to face his punishment and turn his life around. He had just one request: could he go home and see his mother for one night? The commander looked at the broken teenager in front of him and agreed. Francis promised to be at the police station at nine o'clock the following morning.

He kept his word. He went home and spent one last night with his mother. In the morning he had a bath and put on clean clothes, then went to straight to the police station to complete his prison sentence. The punishment had not changed his heart—it was the power of God.

In Popondetta in 1989, the commander of Corrective Institutions Services heard Charles preach. He went to the local mayor and told him, "All the prisoners need to hear this!" The mayor agreed. That night they opened the doors of the prison. All the prisoners—over a hundred men, including all the most dangerous offenders—walked for an hour to the field to hear Charles preach. It was dark and no one was chained or handcuffed, but not one prisoner tried to escape. By the end of the service many were in tears, repenting of their past wrongdoing and praying to God for forgiveness. Many decided to commit their lives to Jesus. Then the whole group walked back to the prison and calmly returned to their cells. Not one prisoner was missing.

Miracle after miracle happened in Lae in 1990. Several people who were deaf in both ears had their hearing restored and some mute people spoke for the first time. An old man came forward with a serious infection which had made him blind and God restored his sight completely that night.

Michael came forward to ask for prayer. He had damaged abdominal muscles and a crooked back. One of the team members asked him, "Do you believe God can heal you?" Michael said he did. "Well, the Bible says that according to your faith it will be done to you." Immediately Michael was able to stand straight for the first time in years.

He later confessed that, as well as working as a mechanic, he had been making illegal guns for the gangs. He gave up his illicit trade and became a preacher and evangelist in Lae.

In Lae, gang members came forward in tears, bringing their guns and laying them down. One gang leader came forward with his arm in plaster. He told how police had shot him because he was a raskol but now he wanted to change his life.

Other gang members who came to the meetings did not come forward for prayer. Charles was keenly aware of these men, lingering in the darkness at the edge of the crowds. He and others in the team invited the men to come back during the daytime so they could talk and ask questions. Former raskols from the Halfway House spent time with them, with the result that another fifteen gang members committed their lives to Jesus. Immediately they wanted to share the news all over town, so they went to shopping centers and marketplaces to tell their stories. Amazed crowds gathered to hear these men as they talked about how wonderful Jesus was. Many more came to the night meetings after hearing them.

After the crusades had finished, most of these men joined different churches in Lae. Their lives continued to be challenging. The man who had been shot by police spoke fearlessly to others in his old gang. Some were so furious they held a gun to his head, demanding he return to his old life with them. He responded by thrusting his Bible in their faces. They backed off and apologized.

Many of the men were on the run from the police, with outstanding charges against them. After their conversion, they went to the police to give themselves up. The authorities were so startled at this uncharacteristic behavior that they decided to trust the power of the conversions and released some of the men without charge. The national newspaper in Port Moresby, the *Post Courier*, printed a letter signed by sixty former raskols:

> Our sincere and heartfelt apologies to the Lae community, individuals, business houses, the provincial authorities, the police department, and the nation of Papua New Guinea, for the violence, unrest, and criminal activities we contributed. Please forgive us. To our brothers in the Police Force, we would like you to Tanim Bel [repent] too. Do not rely too much on your guns and boots.

Part 3 | Opening the Eyes of the Blind

You can change a person's face and body pretty well, but you will never change the heart. Only Jesus can.[63]

Charles was determined to spread the message that Jesus is not a white man's God, a fantasy, or just a religious activity. He truly saw this demonstrated in Lae, and one white missionary later commented, "I have never seen a national man used in that way. And how blessed we were by them!"[64]

After the Lae campaign, Charles had two large bags filled with all the guns handed in. He took them to the then Prime Minister, Rabbie Namaliu. Mr. Namaliu was startled.

"How did you get all this?"

Charles explained the story.

"The police spend so much time and money on efforts to reduce crime—and you just do it like this?"

Charles said it was the power of Jesus. From that time, Mr. Namaliu became the patron of the Halfway House.

In 1989 *Niugini Nius* ran the headline MIRACLES IN MOUNT HAGEN. The report featured stories of an old man, blind for many years, whose sight was restored, and a deaf man who was suddenly able to hear. People who had been unable to walk threw away their crutches and walked freely. Thousands came to the gatherings day after day, despite winds and rain. The reporter quoted one observer's comment, "I've never seen anything like it. Jesus Christ is real!"[65]

Papua New Guinean tradition has always been rich in ceremony and symbolism, and Charles and his team sought creative new ways of bringing Christianity to life. The Wewak crusade in 1991 was officially opened by the Minister for Justice, Bernard Narokobi. There was a torch procession through the streets, attracting thousands of spectators and arriving at the oval in time for the beginning of the crusade. A helicopter landed, bringing a Bible. These events symbolized the coming of the pioneer missionaries who brought God's Word to Papua New Guinea, and looked forward to the future spreading of the gospel by means of modern transport and technologies. The people of Wewak loved it.

Thousands attended the meetings. Sorcerers handed over their implements of witchcraft. Some wept as they told of things they had done, including cursing, and killing people.

---

63. Letters to the Editor, *Post Courier*, 12 November 1990.
64. *Operation Tanim Bel: Lae Crusade*, 7.
65. *Niugini Nius*, 27 October 1989, 18.

One woman came forward to say she had been delivered from nightmares and now realized she had been a victim of witchcraft. Night after night she had been surrounded by people in spirit form, threatening her. She lived in constant terror. One night the spirits in her dream said they were going to kill her, and she cried out to God. The next day she went to the crusade and heard about Jesus. People there prayed for her and she went home that night changed. She slept all night without nightmares and she never experienced those night terrors again.

The gangs continued to come. One night, two groups came forward to give up their weapons. One notorious leader, Buli, who had founded gangs in various cities, decided to turn his life over to Jesus and came forward to make a public apology.

A tense moment arose when a gang group came forward carrying a long box covered in a white cloth. No one knew what was going to happen and Charles wondered if they were bringing him a body. When they drew back the cloth, the box was full of weapons and implements of sorcery. "Charles likened the power behind their crimes to a cooking fire in which the boys were being steadily 'cooked' by the powers of witchcraft."[66]

These stories spread throughout the region until even gangs who were too far away to come sent word that they wanted to give up their guns and hand themselves in. On the final night of the crusade, all the weapons which had been handed in were given to the Chief of Police.

66. *Operation Tanim Bel: Lae Crusade*, 1990, 13.

26

The shooting

CHARLES AND LUCILLE TRUSTED God's protection, but their work was still dangerous.

One night Charles was out in his car when he found himself surrounded by ten armed men who demanded his car keys. He called loudly on the name of Jesus. The leader, who had been trying to grab the keys, was struck dumb, and suddenly all the raskols just stood like dead men, apparently unable to move. Charles drove off. When he was safely away, he looked back and saw them beginning to chase after him, but he was out of reach.

On another night, after Charles and Lucille had gone to bed, there were shouts and noises outside the Halfway House. Charles got up to see what was happening. A group of fifteen or more men were outside the women's dormitory. They had bush knives and guns and were trying to break in. The girls were fighting back and shouting.

Charles ran up the road towards the women's dormitory. Later a witness told him a gunman had been waiting outside his house and had followed him. By the time Charles got to the dormitory, all the Halfway House men were already there, racing to confront the intruders. Two shots rang out and Charles fell to the ground. The intruders got scared and ran.

Back in the house, Lucille heard the gunfire. She guessed immediately that Charles had been hit, then someone came running and told her what had happened. Their son, Enoch, grabbed the car keys and ran out of the house. He saw his dad struggling to walk to the car. Enoch knew he had to get his father to hospital as quickly as possible. They helped Charles into the car. Although Enoch was only fifteen years old and had never driven a car on a public road, he got into the driver's seat and they sped off.

The doctors found that one bullet had entered Charles's hip and another had grazed his chest. They needed to remove the bullet, but they did not have the facilities to operate in Port Moresby. They wanted to move him to a hospital in Australia.

The then Prime Minister, Bill Skate, who was highly supportive of Charles's work, heard about the shooting the next day and offered to charter a plane for Charles to be airlifted to Australia. The doctors told Charles that he had a 50/50 chance of survival. Charles told the Prime Minister not to waste taxpayers' money because God would look after him. Mr. Skate said, "I don't understand you. You might die."

Charles was in Port Moresby for a short time while his condition stabilized, then flew to Brisbane at his own expense and was admitted to the Princess Alexandra Hospital. Professor Steven Lynch operated on him and removed the bullet successfully.

Later some of the team came to Charles's bedside. One doctor told Charles and Lucille he was surprised the bullet had not damaged any of the organs. Instead of going in a straight line, it had missed a major artery and bones.

The doctor asked Charles, "What do you do?"

Lucille replied, "He is a minister of the gospel. He is a man of God."

One of the younger doctors said, "That explains why."

Charles and Lucille both believed that God had preserved his life.

Charles recovered and returned home. He knew the man who had shot him, and men from the gangs came to Charles saying they wanted to execute his attacker. Charles said no, they must not touch him. Instead, he sent the man a message of forgiveness, asking him to repent and give himself up within thirty days. The man refused. Later he was involved in a robbery and killed.

Charles's body healed, but it took longer for his mind and emotions to heal. He was frightened at sudden noises, especially gunfire, and not surprisingly felt shaken and weakened by the experience for at least three or four years. He continued to call on God, saying, "Heal my memories and my emotions. Heal the hatred that was brought by the bullet." He understood this experience had the potential to change him and leave him permanently filled with hate and trauma, if he did not deal with it well.

Meanwhile, the story of the shooting spread, and Charles was held in higher esteem than ever.

THE WORK OF THE Jesus Centre Halfway House continued, now supported by the government and foreign embassies, who could see the effectiveness of the work. An Australian called Larry George resigned from a well-paid bank job to take over management of the center. The program was challenging, with a daily schedule of prayer, study and work aimed at developing the young men and women in body, soul, and spirit.

Although there were ongoing law-and-order issues, gradually the power of the raskol gangs began to weaken. Places which had been no-go areas for the police became more law-abiding. Roads where there had been regular gang roadblocks and hold-ups were widened and became safer. Streets which had been raskol strongholds began to see families living a more normal life.

Of course, Charles was just one of many people working in Port Moresby. Many churches were involved in social justice work of all kinds, including medical clinics, education, youth clubs, vocational training programs and women's refuges. Thousands of local people and expatriates from other countries have worked for years to improve living conditions right across the country.

Dr Ferguson from Lifeline saw the need for better housing in Morata, and he introduced Charles to Habitat for Humanity. Habitat set up a base at the Jesus Centre and a series of volunteers from around the world came to live in one of the houses on-site. Charles became the national president of Habitat, and the organization built hundreds of houses around Morata. They demolished tumbledown shacks and replaced them with permanent houses, each with two bedrooms, a shower and toilet, a kitchen, and a verandah. This transformed the whole culture of the neighborhood. Women were no longer afraid to go outdoors and children began to play in the streets.

Port Moresby was beginning to change, and soon people noticed that birds were returning to Morata.

27

Confrontation: 500 gangsters meet the Prime Minister

OVER AND OVER AGAIN, gang leaders told Charles the same stories: "We need money to live. We need jobs. We need a purpose in life." All those things were missing, and they were frustrated and angry because their voices were unheard. The gangs felt that politicians were ready to punish them, but not to address the root issues.

In 1991 a Crime Summit was held in Port Moresby, but even though gang violence was one of the most serious issues addressed, no gang leaders were invited to the table. Charles and others became frustrated when "experts," including international development agencies, advised that even more experts should be commissioned to study the problem. Charles's response was that they did not need more outsiders coming in to do another study at public expense. The gang members were quite capable of speaking for themselves.

Charles spoke often with Prime Minister Rabbie Namaliu as well as other government ministers about the challenges. An idea began to take shape in Charles's mind. Charles was the son of a chief, and he knew the way of the tribes was to deal with issues face to face. If people had a problem, they would go to the chief. They would sit down together in the men's house and share food. They would not talk about the problems over the food—that would be discourteous. They would eat first, talking in friendship. Then, when the meal was finished, they would raise any issues for discussion. Everyone could have their say, everyone could be heard, and the chief and clan leaders would make decisions together. The arrangement was simple, everyone understood it, and it worked.

What if the gang leaders could meet with the Prime Minister? What if they could talk together, face to face, with time to listen and really hear each other's hearts?

Others caught his vision and preparations began. The *Post Courier* newspaper reported, prime minister agrees to meet gang leaders.

> Charles explained: "The boys want to talk to their leaders. Don't forget that it is our custom. If you want to talk to leaders, you talk to them directly. We feel there is no bridge between the government and the boys. Most of them have been threatened, kicked, booted, and thrown in prison. They are on the run night after night. They lose their dignity."[67]

Mr. Namaliu agreed to meet with the gang leaders and the date was fixed for the 5th and 6th of July. The Prime Minister gave his assurance that nothing would happen to any gang leaders who came. The gang leaders trusted Charles, who often said, "Two things are important: truth and trust. If you don't tell people the truth, they will not trust you next time." They agreed to come.

News spread, and on the Friday afternoon, five hundred raskols arrived at Mirigeda, outside Port Moresby. The army set up tents to accommodate them overnight so that there was plenty of time to talk. Looking back later, Charles said that it was a crazy idea—so much could have gone badly wrong. But at the time, things were desperate and something had to be done.

One group after another arrived at the site. The army provided food and the different groups gathered around their own gang leaders. The Attorney-General, Bernard Narokobi, also arrived to stay overnight. Everyone was rather tense as darkness fell. Charles and his team went from one campfire to another, talking to the men and calming them. "This is your chance—don't waste it. If you want something better in the future, don't start any trouble now."

They listened and even allowed the Attorney-General to sit among them, chatting with them and hearing their stories. Somehow, even though the most notorious rival gangs were all there in one place, no fights broke out and the night was peaceful.

---

67. Quoted in Senge, "Prime Minister agrees to meet gang leaders," *Post Courier*, July 1991.

CONFRONTATION: 500 GANGSTERS MEET THE PRIME MINISTER

The following day the meetings began. Prime Minister Namaliu came, along with the Minister for Defense, Ben Sabumai, and other public servants and officials. The conversations were full and frank. Leaders spoke on behalf of their gangs: "Prime Minister, we need jobs. We need money to live. We need decent housing. We can't live like this."

One man after another spoke about the cycle of brutality. A Goipax gang member called James Haru said he had been in and out of jail since he was twelve years old. "Since I have left school, I have survived on stealing. This afternoon I will have to steal. I will steal tomorrow. I steal because I have no job."[68]

He told the Prime Minister about the violence he had experienced at the hands of police and prison warders, who had beaten him with chains, rifle butts and pipes. Even men who wanted to reform often found themselves reverting to violence after repeated brutality from prison staff. None of the police or prison warders had ever been brought to justice.[69]

Various gang leaders wrote letters about their situations: "We have turned to crime because there has been no job to keep us occupied."[70]

"Most of my 300 youth members are unemployed and when we feel there is nothing to do, we turn to crime. I wish to apologies for all that we have done."[71]

Many had ideas about what was needed, ranging from fishing, a clean-a-thon project, a rehabilitation center, carpentry workshop, farming, brickmaking, and a poultry project. Promises were made and government leaders acknowledged the justice of the men's comments.

The meeting came to a climax when one gang leader stood up while the defense minister was speaking. He called out a strange question: "Minister, who do you worship?"

The minister stopped speaking in surprise.

"Minister, we want to know who you worship."

The minister hesitated. "Why do you ask me that?"

"We worship Satan. We want to know who you worship?"

The minister stretched out his hands. "No! You must not worship Satan. I worship Jesus. He is the one you should worship."

---

68. Quoted in letter from President of Era Youth Group.
69. Senge, "Criminals tell PM why they turn against people," *Post Courier*, 8 July 1991.
70. Letter from KGD.
71. Letter from President of Era Youth Group.

He became emotional as he appealed to the young men before him, explaining that Jesus was the one who would bring them life.

The gang leader continued to interrupt and some of his group began to shout their support. But all around them hundreds of other men began to chant, "Jesus! Jesus! Jesus!" Soon the field was full of young men with hands raised, shouting "Jesus!"

For Charles this was a once-in-a-lifetime moment, seeing many of the gang members in Port Moresby all shouting their allegiance to Jesus.

By the end of the day, many raskols decided to lay down their weapons and turn their lives over to God. What had begun as a law-and-order gathering ended up with men changing their hearts. That year about a hundred men joined the Halfway House, and many people saw it as a turning point in breaking the power of the gangs.

This experience confirmed Charles's belief that foreign aid, investment and addressing social issues were not enough. Jobs, money, and housing were important, but for real lasting change the question that needed to be addressed was, "Who do you worship?"

Throughout all the crusades and conferences across the nation, Charles always made it a priority to work with all the churches in every area. One church or organization could never reach a nation. Charles and Lucille's desire was for the entire body of Christ to work together for one purpose: to see people, and ultimately Papua New Guinea as a whole, renewed by the power of the Word of God.

By the late 1990s, Charles felt that it was time to shift focus. The crusades across the nation ended, and he concentrated on building up the Jesus Centre Halfway House, Life Outreach Ministries (LOM) in Morata, and other LOM-affiliated churches in Papua New Guinea and abroad. But his heartbeat and vision remained the same: "to seek and save that which was lost"[72] through the saving gospel of Jesus Christ.

---

72. Luke 19:10.

PART 4

Heal our land

28

A light in Galilee

"As Jesus walked by the Sea of Galilee, he saw Simon and his brother Andrew casting a net into the sea; for they were fishermen. Then Jesus said to them, "Follow me, and I will make you become fishers of men."[73]

IN 1989 CHARLES TOOK a group to Israel to visit the sites where Jesus had lived. They arrived at their hotel beside Lake Galilee in the late afternoon, and Charles went to his room. As he opened the door, he was struck by blinding light and fell to the floor. He gathered himself and entered the room, shielding his eyes.

The still waters of Lake Galilee were reflecting the afternoon sun, like an enormous mirror reflecting blazing light straight into his room. Standing there, Charles was struck by a sense of the presence of God and fell on his knees, overwhelmed by the radiance of God's glory.

As in the past, he heard God's voice. This time the voice welcomed him to Galilee, saying, "This is where I was and I am now." It was a new experience, yet it was the same familiar presence: Jesus, the same yesterday, today and forever.

That night Charles slept wonderfully well, still feeling surrounded by the presence of God. And God's voice came to him in the night.

The voice told him that in the days ahead, God wanted the Third World nations to prepare the way for the coming of Jesus. Charles questioned this, saying that surely it would be the powerful nations like America that would

---

73. Mark 1:14–17.

be most influential in the future. God disagreed. God told him the Third World nations, the people who had been despised in the past, would rise up and be transformed.

Charles asked God, "What are the signs that will confirm this?"

In reply, the Holy Spirit first led him to look in Mark's gospel, at the story of Simon of Cyrene, the man from North Africa who carried the cross for Jesus.[74] God said, "Now I want you, the Third World countries, to usher in my coming."

Then God made clear two signs. He told Charles that in Australia a new prime minister would make a public apology to the Aboriginal people for the way they had been treated. Then there would be a black president in the United States. Through these two events, the reproach that has been on the indigenous peoples of the world, the black races, and the Third World countries, would begin to be lifted. God had seen how many people had been despised and exploited, and His heart had been hurting with them. God's desire was to lift people up, to bring healing, justice, and righteousness to all.

After that encounter, Charles had a new restlessness in him. On his return to Papua New Guinea, he told this story to the church in Morata and also to a crowd in Lae, and the power of God fell in both places: many people came to God and many were healed.

Nearly twenty years later Kevin Rudd replaced John Howard as prime minister of Australia, and in February 2008 he delivered an apology to the country's indigenous people for wrongs committed against them. Many Papua New Guineans wept when they heard the apology speech—they understood better than any white Australians the pain that is caused when a new race and culture begins to dominate first peoples.

Later that year Charles visited the United States and was invited to preach in a large Methodist church in Ohio. The people said to him, "You are a prophet of God. Tell us who will be the next president of the US." He shared what God had told him, saying that the first sign had already been fulfilled, and the next sign would be a black president in the United States. His election would help to remove the reproach of black people in the USA and elsewhere. The crowd went silent, and later some of the listeners told him it would not happen.

---

74. Mark 15:21.

By the end of that year, Barack Obama was running for office, and on 20 January 2009 he was inaugurated as President of the United States of America.

The two signs had come to pass.

From this time, Charles felt that God was leading him into a new phase. He had always had a father's heart for the poor and the lost—now he was developing a heart for his nation.

29

Building a nation

> "We do not wish to become a nation of black Australians. We should bring to the task of modern nation building that special touch that will allow us to build a unique country."
>
> SIR MICHAEL SOMARE[75]

CREATING A FAMILY OR a new city is one thing; creating a new nation seems impossibly complex. In 1975 Papua New Guinea was granted independence, but it was a land with hundreds of tribes and languages, living in communities which had been physically and socially isolated from each other for thousands of years. The people had been governed by a series of European nations, each with different agendas.

We cannot look at the whole history of Papua New Guinea here, but it is important to acknowledge the exceptional contribution of men like Sir Michael Somare, Sir Tei Abal, Sir Albert Maori Kiki, Sir John Guise, John Momis, Sir Paulius Matane, Sir Julius Chan, Paias Wingti, Sir Rabbie Namaliu and many others as they achieved the seemingly impossible task of establishing Papua New Guinea as a nation.

Some of the first members of parliament were elected; others were hand-picked by the Australian administration in different regions. In the Wiru valley, Yano Belo was selected to represent Kagua-Erave and Turi Wari represented Ialibu-Pangia. Both men were highly respected tribal leaders who had worked as Pidgin interpreters for the Australians. Like

---

75. Somare, *Sana*, 14.

many other members of that first parliament, they had no formal schooling and spoke little or no English.

In the early years of independence, Charles had little involvement in the politics—he was fully occupied with picking up the pieces of broken lives at grassroots level. However, his work often brought him to the attention of government ministers, police, and justice officials as they saw the value of what he was doing.

He began to appreciate the need for good decisions to be made at government level, establishing sound policies and practices, to build and maintain healthy communities. He became increasingly involved with members of parliament, public officials, and even prime ministers. To some he was a friend and confidante; to others he was a thorn in the flesh as he spoke out against immorality and corruption. The little boy from the jungle began to find a voice in the business of nation building.

30

A Prime Minister with a broken heart

BILL SKATE (LATER SIR William) was Prime Minister from 22 July 1997 to 14 July 1999. He was the son of an Australian father and a local mother from a settlement on the outskirts of Port Moresby. He trained and worked as an accountant before entering politics, eventually becoming Speaker of the House, and gaining a reputation as an outspoken man of the people. He visited the Halfway House and came to respect Charles and his work. Over time, he learned to trust Charles as a loyal friend and wise counsellor.

Mr. Skate became Prime Minister at the height of a bloody conflict on the island of Bougainville, where secessionist issues and billion-dollar international copper mining interests together sparked a decade of horrific and deadly violence. His government negotiated an agreement, paving the way to end the crisis. This was probably the greatest achievement of his leadership.[76]

But Mr. Skate still faced a difficult time in office. The Papua New Guinean Parliament has often been fragmented as there are many small parties, so it is hard for any one party to hold a clear majority. Mr. Skate led a minority government, trying to hold together an assortment of small factions and splinter groups. "Like his predecessors, this first Prime Minister who was raised in the settlements of Port Moresby found PNG politics unforgiving."[77]

He valued Charles's quiet friendship, his listening ear, and his prayers.

Mr. Skate was faced with increasing economic difficulties. The population was growing rapidly and the government was struggling to meet the

---

76. McCormack, *The Sandline Affair*, 292-300.
77. Dorney, *Skate a Victim of PNG Political System*.

needs for health, education, and infrastructure throughout the diverse regions. Government revenues were falling, due to the closure of the Bougainville copper mine, and a drop in market prices for resources such as minerals and logging.[78] Then the situation was made worse by a prolonged drought.

Despite these issues, Bill Skate was loved by many because of his common touch and his reputation for straight-talking. He was known as a hard drinker, telling Charles more than once, "There are two things I like in life. I like to sing and I like a glass of whisky." Charles himself was not a drinker, but he understood Mr. Skate's genuine heart for his people and he knew that the Prime Minister was a man under extreme pressure.

The Skate government became increasingly turbulent and seemed to be losing control of many social and economic issues. There was a moment when Mr. Skate reached a personal breaking point.

One night Charles and Lucille were about to go to sleep. It was midnight. They heard footsteps on the wooden stairs outside their house, then a knock. Charles opened the door and found Bill Skate standing there, looking like a broken man. They sat on the veranda in the darkness and the Prime Minister poured out his grief.

He told how he had held so much hope when he came to power. "I wanted to lead a government that was honest, to clean out corruption, to build a team who would care about the people."

He told Charles that he had chosen men whom he thought he could trust, but now he did not think he could trust anyone. He had recently discovered that several of his ministers had been involved in sexual affairs with young girls. At first, he had not believed the rumors, but then he challenged the men and they admitted the stories were true. Hard on the heels of that shock, he discovered that those men and others had been siphoning off millions of kina into their own pockets.

The Prime Minister sat on Charles's verandah and wept. He eventually went home and picked up the reins again, but he began to have heart problems. Physically and emotionally, his heart could no longer carry the weight of his task, and less than two years after taking office, he resigned. About six years later, he suffered a massive stroke and died at the age of fifty-two.

Leadership of a developing nation was a daunting task. Every one of Papua New Guinea's prime ministers has faced these problems, and there have been no easy answers.

78. Standish, *The Skate Era*.

31

A Speaker speaks

"It's tough being a politician in Papua New Guinea." Francis Marus should know. He made this comment after ten years of experience as a member of parliament, representing the people of Kimbe in West New Britain.

For some politicians, including Francis, Charles has been more than a friend—he is like a father. Mr. Marus became a highly respected MP. In the past, however, his life was headed in a different direction.

Francis's parents were from Sepik, then they moved to the island of West New Britain in the 1960s when the government was offering land for small farmers to start oil palm plantations. Francis's father took up the opportunity and became a settler, hoping for a better life for his family. So Francis was born in a place where his family were "immigrants," speaking a different language and racially and culturally different from the people around them. It was not always easy.

For generations, young boys all over Papua New Guinea moved easily from childhood into manhood. As small children they lived with their mothers and siblings in the women's houses. Then at adolescence they moved into the men's house where, in the familiar setting of their village and tribe, they were taught everything they needed to know. They learned how to hunt, maintain gardens, build their houses, and organize the activities of their family and village. "Men learned about life itself."[79]

When the Marus family moved to a different region, suddenly all the familiar ways were gone. The language, the customs and the culture were strange and there was no village or tribe to train the young Marus boys.

---

79. Francis Marus, private interview, August 2015.

Francis felt this keenly. Like many others, he became lost in a mixed culture with uncertain influences. He finished primary school, but by the time he was thirteen, he was involved in all sorts of trouble. He went out every morning, but instead of going to school he went off with his friends. By year eight, he was expelled from school.

From this point, life went downhill. There was nothing to stop him from getting into more trouble—petty theft, small acts of violence—"just trying to prove to your peer group that you are a man." Francis remembered vividly how the words of his friends, "You are a woman! You are a coward!" pushed him further into a lifestyle of rebellion.

Francis moved away from his family and followed some friends to East New Britain, where he continued to mix with the wrong people. "I just wanted to prove to that group that I could survive." He was involved with the police many times and eventually found himself in a police lock-up, charged with armed robbery and murder.

While he was in jail on remand, he heard that his mother had died. He spent a week in a hot concrete police cell, without food, and it was the worst week of his life. At the end of that week, he heard a knock on the door. A man walked in. He sat down beside Francis and gave him two large bread rolls filled with salad and meat, and a carton of juice.

Francis took a bite and it tasted like the most delicious food in the world. He said to the visitor, "I want to work for you."

The man said, "But I am a pastor." The man who was showing him kindness was Pastor Albert Luckies, who worked for the Life Outreach Ministries Church in Kimbe.

"I don't care. My current life, the underworld life, hasn't fed me for a week. Please, I want to work for you when I get out of here."

They spoke for a long time, and later Francis said, "I met Jesus in prison."

He was sentenced to four-and-a-half years in jail for his part in the robbery, but within a few weeks the sentence was overturned. Much to his surprise, he was released on probation. He had been in and out of prison before, but this time it was different—he felt changed inside.

Francis joined the Halfway House in Kimbe, one of several rehabilitation centers that Life Outreach Ministries had set up around the country. He was mentored by Pastor Albert and other Christian people and successfully completed his schooling. Francis had made a commitment to give every part of his life to God and he did not want to turn back. He also found time to work alongside Pastor Albert and other leaders, encouraging young men to leave their gangs and criminal lives. Many lads listened and followed Francis out of the gangs. He knew how bad life could be, and he wanted the young men to experience something better, saying,

"I don't just want heaven in the next life. I want to see heaven on earth now."

In 1995 he went to university in Australia and then trained to become a helicopter pilot. When he returned home, his father was astonished and delighted at the change in his son. The people in their community also marveled at the transformation. They all knew about Francis's previous life, but now they saw leadership potential in him.

Somewhat to his surprise, he was nominated as a candidate for the 2002 elections. Francis was particularly interested in issues surrounding the indigenous people and non-indigenous settlers in his region, and he agreed to stand.

He had no previous background or experience in politics, but he attracted a significant share of the vote, coming third. He decided to stay in the district, living and working there to build relationships with the people and to develop a sound understanding of local issues.

He stood as a candidate again in the 2007 elections and won. He felt humbled by that victory, and ascribed it to God. He felt deeply connected to God throughout that period, as if God's hand was on his shoulder, and God's voice was saying it was His timing. He moved to Port Moresby to take up his new role. Charles met him there and took the young politician under his wing. To Charles, Francis was always "one of our boys" and Francis looked up to Charles as a father.

For Francis, entering Papua New Guinean politics was tough. He was the son of an immigrant farmer, and he was very conscious of his own troubled past. In addition, there were the problems facing all politicians in a very new nation. In most Western democracies, the parliamentary systems have developed over hundreds of years: the structures and processes are well established and the whole population more or less understands the system. Papua New Guinea moved from what was virtually a stone-age tribal system, to colonial administration, then to an independent parliamentary democracy in little more than a generation.

It is not surprising that there have been problems—the real wonder is that, within a few decades, the entire parliament, public service, judiciary, and all sections of local government have shifted from colonial authority to being run completely by local Papua New Guineans. A modern nation has been birthed, and has survived.

Francis often felt overwhelmed, but he said what gave him courage was remembering that Papua New Guineans had always been able to go into the men's house to discuss problems and find solutions. He often said to himself as he walked into the parliament building, "I can do this—this is just our man-house. We know how to do this."

Francis met with Charles often, relying on him for guidance, encouragement, and wisdom. As well as being a man of God, Charles was a chief and the son of a chief, and he understood how to lead people. Charles often reminded Francis of God's call, saying, "It was a miracle how God found you. So many of your comrades died, but you turned to Christ."

For a young politician, it meant the world to have Charles's fatherly hand on his shoulder, and his quiet voice saying, "I go with you, my son."

In his second term, Francis became Deputy Speaker, elected unopposed. In the days ahead, he was to play a pivotal role in a moment of national crisis.

32

Peace on earth

CHARLES CONTINUED HIS WORK in Port Moresby, and although he no longer ran evangelism campaigns, he kept close contact with other pastors and community leaders across Papua New Guinea. He was driven by the conviction that politics, education, and economics alone were not enough to create a cohesive nation. There needed to be a spiritual element to form and maintain strong communities.

Charles had seen over and over again that real faith could change criminal behavior and gang violence, not by outward rules but by changing a person from within. What about tribal wars and revenge killings, which continued to plague many regions of Papua New Guinea? Charles and many other Christian leaders continued to work with village leaders and churches, teaching them the ways of Jesus, believing that warfare would cease when hearts and minds were changed.

After the crusades in Mount Hagen, Charles visited the region often, supporting and encouraging leaders and local people in their work to end violence. During that time, he saw one place where faith reshaped a district—where people stopped seeing the enemy as the enemy and began to see them as brothers.

The Highlands Highway through the Nebilyer Valley, west of Mount Hagen, was one of the most notorious roads in the world. Poor construction and inadequate maintenance were not the only hazards: for years drivers risked mud, landslides, and potholes, avoiding huge logging trucks, only to find themselves held up at roadblocks and robbed at gunpoint. Policing these remote areas was virtually impossible as the police had neither the manpower nor resources to deal with the problem.

One section of the road was particularly dangerous because two warring tribes waged constant hostilities in a vicious cycle of revenge killings. As soon as villages were rebuilt, they were burned down again. People suffered because animals were killed or stolen, crops were destroyed and their land was often blackened and useless. Families were tired of having to run away every time there was a new outbreak of violence.

One day Charles and Lucille were driving through the valley. On a hill to their left, they could see smoke from burning villages, and the landscape was desolate. Huge rocks blocked the road and as soon as they slowed down, men with guns and bush knives surrounded their car. Charles wound down the window and asked what they were doing. The men recognized Charles and apologized, backing off and waving them through. Others were not so fortunate.

Pastors such as Andrew Laip from Mount Hagen worked in this area for years, presenting the gospel of Jesus, explaining repentance, forgiveness, and the need for salvation. Some people began to hear the words and believe them. Charles continued to offer his support and encouragement, even when it seemed the warfare and violence would never end.

Nambuka Mara was a chief in the Nebilyer Valley (he had been the first premier of Western Highlands from 1978 to 1984). He too was sick and tired of the destructive violence in his region. He organized a rally with all the tribal leaders of the valley and asked Charles to come and speak. On the second night, Nambuka Mara and a group of chiefs came to Charles with a large bundle wrapped in banana leaves. "We are bringing you something," he said. "I want you to look at it and pray for it."

Charles was a little nervous, not knowing what it could be. But the whole crowd was watching, so he opened it.

Inside was a pile of soil. The chief explained, "Can you pray for our soil and break the curse? So much blood has been shed on our land that we feel it is cursed and we want our land to be healed. Then our plantations, our gardens, our food, and our people will be healed. I will distribute the soil to our leaders, and each one will take some soil and throw it on their land, and we will have healing."

Charles prayed, calling on God to bless and heal the land, and then he gave the bundle back to the chief. Everyone was weeping as the chief took the bundle of soil. He gave a small handful to each of the local leaders, who took it back to their lands. It was a powerful symbol, and the leaders and people believed that this was a significant moment in their pathway to peace and wholeness in the valley.

In 2013 Charles and Lucille returned to this area. They saw beautiful forests, neat houses, and lush market gardens. Charles exclaimed in amazement and stopped the car. A man was working in his garden and came to greet them while a young mother emerged from a house carrying a smiling baby. Other small children came running, peeping shyly from behind their mother's skirt. It was a scene of peace and rural prosperity.

Charles asked what had been happening and the man told the story.

Many of the people from their tribe had been disgusted at the ongoing war and violence. They began to pray, seeking God's help to bring peace. They made a commitment to God and to each other that they would not kill or seek revenge, but work for peace and forgiveness, no matter what. Their leaders went to the enemy tribe and explained that they were not going to fight again—they wanted peace.

There was an uneasy quiet for a time, then the enemy tribe decided to test their resolve. The enemies kidnapped two of the tribe's young men and killed them.

The group who had committed to peace met together in great distress. They prayed long and hard, and decided that they must not seek revenge. They had to show the way of forgiveness. Instead of revenge killings and burning, they would go to their enemies with gifts. Instead of seeking compensation, they would give the equivalent in money and gifts to the killers. They collected thousands of kina and several pigs, worth thousands of dollars.

They approached the enemy tribe, bearing their gifts. They explained to them that they were now following a different way, the way of Jesus, who said, "Forgive your enemies. Love those who mistreat you." They said that instead of retaliating, killing, and destroying, they wanted to bless them, and they handed over the money and pigs.

Their love broke their enemies. The enemy tribe was defeated not by guns and arrows, but by forgiveness, gentleness, and peace. They laid down their weapons and renounced violence. Since then, the valley has been thriving: crops grow, the forest has regenerated, children are healthier and there is life.

Charles knew he had been right: if they wanted to see thriving communities, leaders needed to pay attention to the healing of the spirit.

The events in Nebilyer Valley are not an isolated example. A young woman in the Halfway House in Port Moresby told an equally astonishing story. Her name is Josephine.

Josephine came from a small village from a part of the Western Highlands where there had been constant tribal warfare. For two years, no one in her village had slept properly. Often a woman would collapse to her knees in the middle of the day, weeping in grief and exhaustion. They kept saying, "One day! One day we will live in a peaceful place." Church leaders tried to teach a different way, but the strife continued.

One Saturday night, Josephine, then about fifteen years old, woke in the early hours of the morning. She looked outside and saw a crowd of armed men surrounding her house, holding bows, spears, and guns. She picked up her guitar and began to pray and sing, worshipping God quietly in the darkness. There was a loud knock at the door. Josephine opened it and a man with a gun stood in the doorway, demanding that her father come out. She shouted at him. To her surprise, the men all ran away, though some turned back and fired shots at the house.

Josephine's mother gathered the women of the village together and they began to meet regularly to pray for peace. Eventually they decided to take their prayers directly to the main battleground. They fasted for three days, then as a group they set off at midnight to walk to the battlefield, about 40 kilometers away.

Josephine and the other women were scared all through that night journey. They reached the battleground and could see the enemy warriors hiding among the trees. The women walked into the middle of the cleared ground and knelt in full view of the enemy. They cried out to God for two hours and then quietly stood up and walked home.

They continued to do this for several months. Every time they were scared, because they were surrounded by the men who had killed their husbands, brothers, and sons. There were times when the enemy shot at them, but the women continued to pray.

After several months, the men of both tribes laid down their weapons. Both sides acknowledged their wrongdoing and offered peace, but it was not easy. A local pastor called Joseph Kangal helped them through the process, and whole tribes repented and burned their weapons. After three hard years, peace was restored.

Forgiveness was difficult, and many people struggled to extend it to their former enemies. Josephine tells the story best:

> Now people realize that they have done wrong. The whole tribe has repented and they gave the land to God. Now I can see things are starting to change since the repentance. Since the tribe gave the whole district to the Lord, we now have education, roads, power, and a good community. Now whole villages have permanent houses.[80]

For yours is the kingdom, the power, and the glory.

Josephine and the farmers of the Nebilyer Valley demonstrated that God's principles work. If we want to defeat violence, stronger violence is not the answer. It may work for a time, but the only long-lasting solution is the power of forgiveness, the renunciation of violence and revenge, and a commitment to love instead of hate. That was how Jesus himself "absorbed violence, even death."[81]

> Forgiveness opens the way. We need to be caught up in a spirit of forgiveness. If that is successful, that opens the way for justice to flow. Our forgiveness releases us. We are not victimized by our own anger and guilt or torment, because we have forgiven. And it releases the spirit in us to be able to reach out for dialogue and relationship to begin. It allows the possibility to be free from resentment, so we do not carry deep down bitterness and resentment into the pathway going forward.[82]

The power of forgiveness and love does change the world. Charles had seen it in the gangs, and among the warring tribes in the Highlands. He knew that Jesus could bring life, and that this kind of love could bring unity to a fragmented nation.

---

80. Josephine Karl, *private interview*, Port Moresby, July 2012.
81. Costello, *Thine be the Kingdom*.
82. Paulson, *Forgive us our sins*.

33

Kings and priests

> And they sang a new song, saying, "You are worthy to take the scroll and to open its seals, for you were killed, and at the cost of your own blood you have purchased for God persons from every tribe, language, people, and nation. You have appointed them as kings and priests to serve our God, and they will reign on the earth."[83]

CHARLES KEPT IN CLOSE contact with the people in the Wiru valley. Although he lived in Port Moresby, he was still his people's chief and they recognized his authority. They knew that he was a man of influence in Port Moresby, and they trusted him. Some of his fellow leaders asked him to represent the Pangia-Ialibu district in parliament, but Charles said no—his work was to be a man of God. Instead, he recommended they approach his cousin, Peter O'Neill, the son of Australian patrol officer Brian O'Neill. After much thought, Mr. O'Neill agreed and stood for election in Pangia-Ialibu in 2002, leaving behind a successful business career. He was elected and in his first term became a government minister.

From the beginning, Mr. O'Neill was highly regarded in his own electorate. The people saw the difference he made to their district: funds did not disappear, roads, schools and health services were built and well maintained, and the community learned to trust him. He was re-elected

---

83. Revelation 5:9–10

in 2007. Charles continued to be a friend and sometimes an advisor to his younger cousin.

In 2011, four American men who were highly regarded as "prophets"[84] came to Port Moresby, to spend three days at a conference with Christian leaders from all the major churches in Papua New Guinea. On the Saturday night, one of the men, Dr Bill Hamon, pointed in a particular direction and told everyone to pray. The crowd of over two thousand people pointed in that direction and prayed in tongues. The Americans did not know what they were pointing at, but Charles and most of the other Papua New Guineans realized they were all pointing directly at the National Parliament building nearby.

The prayer became intense—those there said it was like being in the middle of a raging battle. The same thing happened on the Sunday. After an hour of ferocious prayer, Dr Hamon suddenly cried, "Change!" Another prophet declared, "A new nation will be birthed in a day!"

What did it mean—what was going to change? Soon after this, there was a change of government.

Things had been heating up in parliament for some time. The Grand Chief, Sir Michael Somare, was in his third term as Prime Minister, and faced allegations of corruption and increasing dissatisfaction with his leadership.

Francis Marus was the Deputy Speaker by this time and he was invited to join a move against Sir Michael. Francis kept thinking of the Bible story in which David refused to rise against King Saul because he knew that God had appointed Saul as king. Francis decided not to join the push against the Prime Minister, believing that if Sir Michael had done wrong, then it was better to let God deal with him.

Then Sir Michael collapsed with a heart attack and was taken to Singapore for treatment. After several months in hospital and further heart surgery, it became clear he would not be able to resume his duties for some time. Deputy Prime Minister Sam Abal continued as Acting Prime Minister, but there was much unrest, with further allegations about corruption and cronyism. Arthur Somare, Sir Michael's son, announced that the family had decided their father should retire.

The Opposition brought a motion that Sir Michael be removed from office on medical grounds. According to the Papua New Guinean

---

84. In the Bible, a "prophet" is a person with a gift of insight, who can discern God's thoughts in a situation, rather than someone who can foretell the future.

Constitution, this would allow the election of a new Prime Minister. The Speaker, Jeffrey Nape, accepted the motion and the Opposition leader, Beldan Namah, nominated Peter O'Neill for Prime Minister. A vote was taken and O'Neill was elected as the new Prime Minister on 2 August 2012.[85]

Meanwhile, Sir Michael recovered and was outraged. He returned to Papua New Guinea and won a Supreme Court judgment that the election of Mr. O'Neill had been unconstitutional. He rallied his own supporters and prepared to return to his role as Prime Minister.

By this time, the Speaker had resigned and Francis Marus was the Acting Speaker. He found himself presiding over a House in the middle of a constitutional crisis, with two rival prime ministers, two governors-general and two police chiefs all claiming authority. He was presented with the Supreme Court ruling in favor of Sir Michael and had a sleepless night praying and weighing up the situation.

But in the morning, he felt the decision was clear. Previously he had refused to join the backstabbing of Sir Michael, believing that God should be the judge. Now, he saw that Sir Michael had been removed from office already by the issues of his health, and he felt that Mr. O'Neill was the right man to lead the country into the future. This was not an easy decision as Francis did not belong to Mr. O'Neill's party. Also, the Marus family and Sir Michael were all from the Sepik region, and in Papua New Guinea *wantoks*[86] generally stick together. However, Francis believed that Mr. O'Neill was a capable and honest man who was committed to the good of the nation and the removal of corruption.

The next morning, Francis walked into the parliament chamber, sat in the Speaker's chair, and declared the House open for business, acknowledging Mr. O'Neill as the legitimate Prime Minister.

Charles prayed with the new Prime Minister: "Prime Minister, love God with all your heart, with all your soul and with all your spirit. Love God and love our 7.5 million people fairly. Your destiny will be guided by the Word of God. He will give you wisdom to lead the nation."

Mr. O'Neill received strong support from many parties. The people of Papua New Guinea were heartily tired of corruption and mismanagement and so were many politicians. He soon gathered around himself a group of

---

85. May, *Papua New Guinea's 'Political Coup'*

86. *Wantok*, literally "one talk," means someone who shares the same language or comes from the same place.

men who were committed to cleaning up the government, and their numbers grew steadily.

Behind the scenes, the Prime Minister set up working groups to establish policies, guidelines, and processes across all areas of government, aiming to make it harder for members of parliament and other officials to misappropriate funds. Because of Charles's reputation as a man of integrity, he was invited to work with various groups as they sought to build strong ethical foundations. Mr. O'Neill also streamlined financial practices to make government money easier to trace. He was the first Prime Minister to visit every district across the country, and he often turned up unexpectedly, asking detailed questions about projects, and checking that funds were being used properly.

Other MPs spoke highly of the new standards of integrity and professionalism and felt there was a new spirit in parliament. Of course, not everyone was happy and there was fierce opposition from some. Inevitably issues arise, mistakes happen and not everything goes smoothly.

In the tiny village where Charles' mother, Lendepame was born, a tribal leader prayed, "Who are we, that from our tribe has come a man of God, and now a prime minister. Who are we, that from the womb of our tribe has come godliness!"

WHEN MR. O'NEILL CAME to office, plans were already underway for a National Day of Prayer and Repentance, and in 2011 he officially declared 26 August as a national annual holiday. The reaction in foreign media was puzzlement, but Papua New Guineans seemed largely supportive. Charles and his fellow church leaders saw it as an important day, when members of parliament could lead the nation in a national *Haus krai,* a day of confession of mistakes, repentance, and renewal.

The Speaker of Parliament, Theo Zurenuoc, spoke about the importance of this day:

> We are spiritual beings; we are eternal spiritual beings operating out of a temporary physical form. Prime Minister, you have led this nation to humble itself before the Lord, and to repent, to give thanksgiving and praise before the Lord this day. You and your leaders have given the Lord a space in the heart of the democracy of our nation—the Parliament."[87]

---

87. Zurenuoc, *Prayer and Repentance Day Speech*, 36–37.

The Prime Minister was equally open in acknowledging the role of spirituality in the politics of the nation: "Today we are here to praise and acknowledge and honor our good Lord Jesus Christ, and the work that he continues to do and look after in our country."[88]

Many Western commentators find this difficult to understand, but the underlying concept is highly attractive. Imagine it for a moment: the prime minister or president of a country and parliamentarians have an annual day set aside when they lead the way in acknowledging past mistakes, examining their own actions and hearts, confessing, and repenting of wrongdoing, and then seeking to find better ways of moving forward. Most of us would like to see that, especially if it was done without political point-scoring between the parties.

In 2014, thousands of people turned out before dawn, standing in the rain outside the parliament building for hours to pray. Later in the day, at a Prayer Luncheon in the State Function Room of the National Parliament, Mr. O'Neill spoke to the nation:

> The challenges we are facing are not new. Many of us know about challenges, we have faced challenges throughout our life.
>
> For me in particular, I had challenges very early in life, even before I was born, when my mother was a very young pregnant woman even considering abortion. There were challenges in the very remote area where Pastor Charles and I come from, trying to get an education, trying to survive in a very difficult environment.
>
> So, I think that it is important in the calendar of the nation that we must have a day like today when we repent and we honor and praise our good Lord.
>
> I am certain that with your prayers and with your guidance, that this nation is destined for greater things. Many times, we have been talked down, made to feel that we are incapable, to feel inferior. But I can tell you that Papua New Guinea is now standing at the cusp of a brighter future. As we enter the 40th year of independence—we are going to build a new chapter.
>
> Despite the many differences that we may have, it is better for the nation if we remain together. So that is why I want to announce to you, every year if we are in government, we will have a joint national public holiday so that it gives us a time to reflect."[89]

---

88. Zurenuoc, *Prayer and Repentance Day Speech*, 38.
89. O'Neill, *Concluding Address*.

After the luncheon, parliament sat for its afternoon session. A member of parliament from each region prayed and repented on behalf of his own region. Some were weeping as they asked God to heal, restore and transform their provinces and deliver them from the sins of the past.

After the first National Day of Prayer and Repentance, Charles and the leaders of most of the main churches in Port Moresby began to meet regularly to pray and fast. They realized that if they wanted to make a difference in their society, they needed to be united. They formed a group known as the "Body of Christ" under a team of leaders representing most of the major churches. At first some denominations were wary, but by 2015 virtually all churches in PNG were involved, led by Pastor Joseph Walters and Dr Michael Wilson.

Charles and other church leaders now saw Papua New Guinea as a "kingdom nation." In the Bible, nations were at their best when the "kings" (political leaders) worked together with the "priests and prophets" (spiritual leaders). If God's principles of governance were truly at work, he believed, there would be a society of righteousness, justice, peace, and love. God's kingdom crosses all human boundaries because it is a message of unity, with no barriers of tribe, race, class, wealth, status, or gender. Jesus brought people together who would normally stay apart and brought healing to damaged relationships.

Charles has a vision of a community which represents God's kingdom on earth. This is not some oppressive type of religious nationalism—rather, it is a vision of a society ordered according to the principles of heaven.

"Your kingdom come": a society where there is love, equity, justice, and peace.

34

Crossing into the promised land

IN SEPTEMBER 2015 PAPUA New Guinea celebrated its 40th year of independence. The majority of Papua New Guineans now identify as Christian, and many, including Charles, saw this anniversary as a spiritually significant time.

In the Bible story, the people of Israel were in slavery in Egypt, and then spent forty years wandering in the desert before crossing over the Jordan River to enter their Promised Land. Many Papua New Guinean Christians believe that their 40th anniversary marked a crossing into their own "promised land," entering a new season of fruitfulness. After a challenging forty years, they believe they are now moving into an era of blessing, prosperity, and peace. This is not a consumerist version of prosperity, implying idleness and material wealth based on exploitation of others: it carries the sense of thriving. They see a society where people can work productively and thrive in every sense, living in healthy relationships with themselves, with each other and with their environment.

In June 2014 Dr Bill Hamon returned to Port Moresby. This time, he addressed church, business and political leaders and made a prediction about the nation.

> I have travelled all over the world, and what I am about to say, I have never said to any nation. You have gone through struggles; you have gone through hardships. But the Holy Spirit would have me declare this: that Papua New Guinea is now the first kingdom nation."[90]

---

90. As reported by Charles and Lucille Lapa and others in attendance.

Part 4 | Heal our land

Some western journalists have noticed the "Christianizing" of Papua New Guinean politics and attributed it to the effect of "American televangelists." But Dr Hamon's speech just confirmed what many local church leaders and people were already saying.

Long before Dr Hamon's statement, there were some intriguing developments. In 2013, the Speaker, Theodore Zurenuoc, announced he was going to remove the totem pole from the Grand Hall of Parliament House and replace it with a "Pillar of National Identity and Unity." He and others saw the totem pole as representing old ways and the divided tribalism of the past, and he believed that the only way to bring national unity was through the Word of God. Foreign media have been critical of Mr. Zurenuoc's actions, but he was not acting alone. At every step he was working as part of a parliamentary house committee, including members of the government and opposition parties.

Charles and other church leaders supported the Speaker, who consulted them in planning the new pillar. Charles remembered the spirit pole that was prepared in the men's house in Kalane when he was a boy, and how his father told him, "One day these things will be gone." Now he was watching a new spirit pole emerge, one which represented new life and the future.

The base of the pole is jasper and represents the Word of God, "the foundation, the eternal source of wisdom, principles and moral conscience."[91] Everything, including the Papua New Guinea Constitution, is guided by the Word of God for the peace, order, and welfare of the people. Rising from the base is a tall pillar known as the "Unity Pole" with the word unity inscribed in each of Papua New Guinea's more than 840 languages.

Of course, there has been opposition from various groups, but most church leaders and Christians support it. They believe that this new pole is a powerful symbol of the living Word, which can guide the parliament and the people and bring about a deeper respect for God. They expect that the result will be greater wisdom in decision-making, greater unity, and a decline in corruption.

In 2014, while all these plans were being made, Dr Gene Hood from Indiana, USA, visited Papua New Guinea. He was a minister, missionary, and philanthropist who had supported mission work in many parts of the world.

Dr Wilson, one of the leaders of the "Body of Christ" group, heard that Dr Hood was in the country and travelled to the Highlands to meet him.

---

91. Theodore Zurenuoc, *Unity Pole*.

Dr Wilson told Dr Hood about what was happening in the nation and in the parliament.

Dr Hood was deeply moved. "I have never heard anything like this in my life." He told Dr Wilson he had a Bible in his book collection, one of the original King James Bibles from 1611. "Your story hits me in the heart. I will give this Bible as my gift to your nation."[92]

In April 2015, the Speaker of Parliament led a delegation to the United States and they were presented with the priceless Bible by Dr Hood. A few days later, Dr Hood died. It was as if his work was now complete.

On the day the delegation returned to Papua New Guinea, thousands of people filled the airport. Charles and other church leaders were there and Prime Minister O'Neill, the Opposition leader, Don Polye, and the Speaker, Theo Zurenuoc, accepted the Bible on behalf of the nation.

Then a convoy carried the Bible through the streets of Port Moresby. Thousands of people lined the streets, throwing flowers in front of the procession and shouting, "Welcome! Welcome!" They were welcoming Jesus into the capital city of their nation. It was just like the biblical story of people welcoming Jesus into Jerusalem, throwing palm leaves along his path.

On the day of the 40th anniversary of Independence, 16 September 2015, the Bible was officially brought to Parliament House. Thousands of people dressed in the national colors of Papua New Guinea started to fill the streets from three o'clock in the morning. Different tribes celebrated together, singing and dancing in the streets as the Bible was carried to Parliament House.

On the steps outside parliament, the Prime Minister, the Speaker, church leaders and Dr Hood's family were all waiting, together with members of parliament. There were powerful speeches, and the crowds cheered in response to Mr. O'Neill's words.

He described the Bible as a national treasure that unified a country of one thousand tribes and tongues. "This book must bond us together and be a uniting force for our country in the years to come, because we have lots of ethnic groups, lots of tribes, lots of languages, but one Bible."[93]

The Speaker, Mr. Zurenuoc, said that bringing the Bible into the parliament "is not about destroying PNG's culture but about having in the House a symbol of our Christian faith. We will remain a culturally diverse people, but we surely will be a strongly knitted nation of one thousand

---

92. As reported by those present.
93. *Post Courier*, 21 September 2015, 7.

tribes bonded together by our faith in God, and that is what we are saying today by paying homage to the Bible."[94]

When the speeches were over, Charles was one of four men who carried the Bible right into the parliament chamber.

Charles's story, like the story of Papua New Guinea, is still being written. In Charles and Lucille's family, new grandchildren have been born. The Halfway House and Life Outreach Ministries continue to operate. In the parliament, financial pressures, political turmoil, and human issues keep arising, and like every nation around the world, Papua New Guinea struggles with local and global challenges. Charles's work is not finished.

Charles sees this as a time of transition for Papua New Guinea. His father, Chief Imbinali, searched for the unknown God beyond the clouds. At the 40th anniversary celebrations, Charles saw that the unknown God had made Himself known—to Charles himself, to the people and even to the government, which had now accepted the Word of God as their National Treasure.

The child called Tiki has become a man. He has preached to thousands. He has seen blind eyes being opened and hearts being changed. He has established churches in Papua New Guinea and abroad, and he has helped to build unity among the churches of his nation. He has travelled around the world.

And, as one of four people chosen out of a population of 7.5 million, with his own hands he helped to carry Jesus into the heart of government.

"I found the God beyond the clouds, and I have totally committed my life to serving Him. I have declared Him to the villages and the raskols, to businessmen and politicians. And now I declare to my nation that this God must be the God of Papua New Guinea. It is my honor to continue to pray for our nation."

In all these things, Tiki continues to fulfil the call that came at Mount Ialibu.

---

94. *Post Courier*, 21 September 2015, 7.

Bibliography

Attenborough, David and Fuller, Errol, *Drawn from Paradise: The Discovery, Art and Natural History of the Birds of Paradise*, Collins, London, 2012.
Ballard, Chris, "The Art of Encounter: Verisimilitude in the Imaginary Exploration of Interior New Guinea, 1725–1876," in Jolly, Tcherkézoff and Tryon (eds), *Oceanic Encounters: Exchange, Desire, Violence*, ANU E Press, 2009, pp. 221ff. <http://press.anu.edu.au/oceanic_encounters/mobile_devices/ch08s06.html>.
Brown, Bill, *Fifty Shades of Kiap*. <http://asopa.typepad.com/asopa_people/2012/12/fifty-shades-of-kiap-of-stayers-players-neer-do-wells.html>.
Cairns Daily Times, The, cited in the *Northern Standard* newspaper, Darwin, Australia, 4 October 1927.
Callick, Rowan, "Highlander with big shoes to fill," *The Australian*, 16 September 2011. <http://www.theaustralian.com.au/news/features/highlander-with-big-shoes-to-fill/story-e6frg6z6-1226138245402?nk=73fa32c954e98a30f38a492b1a1a3b43>.
Circular Instruction No. 147: Subject: Extension of Government Control to Restricted Areas, Department of District Services and Native Affairs, Port Moresby, 3 April 1952.
Costello, Tim, "Thine be the kingdom," 31 March 2015. <https://www.youtube.com/watch?v=8JcUE9nrLGs>.
Cruz, Nicky, *Run Baby Run*, Bridge-Logos Publishers, Gainsville, 1968.
Dorney, Sean, "Skate a victim of PNG political system," *Pacific Islands Report*, Radio Australia, 7 July 1999. <http://archives.pireport.org/archive/1999/july/07-08-01.html>.
Dredge, James, *Brief Notices of the Aborigines of New South Wales Including Port Phillip*, James Harrison, Geelong, 1845.
Hardy, Graham, "The DIY Cadet," *Una Voce*, No. 4, December 2010, p. 22. <http://pngaa.org/site/blog/2015/09/16/the-diy-cadet-graham-hardy>.
Joannes, Nicole, "KJV Bible reaches Parliament," *Post Courier*, 21 September 2015.
Lapa, Charles, *Operation Tanimbel 1984*, Life Outreach Ministries, Boroko, 1984.
Letter from KGD, Horse Camp Block, addressed to Prime Minister, 6 July 1991, on file with the Foundation for Law Order and Justice.
Letter from President of Era Youth Group, addressed to Prime Minister, 6 July 1991.
Letters to the editor, *Post Courier*, 12 November 1990.
McCormack, Timothy L.H. "The 'Sandline Affair': Papua New Guinea Resorts to Mercenarism to End the Bougainville Conflict," *Yearbook of International Humanitarian Law*, 1, 1998, pp. 292–300. <http://journals.cambridge.org/action/displayAbstract?fromPage=online&aid=4044384>.

May, Ron, "Papua New Guinea's 'political coup': The ousting of Sir Michael Somare," *State, Society and Governance in Melanesia*, No. 1, 2011. <http://ips.cap.anu.edu.au/sites/default/files/BriefNote_2011_1_May.pdf>.

McFarlane, S., *Among the Cannibals of Papua New Guinea*, Presbyterian Board of Publication and Sabbath-School Work, 1888. <https://archive.org/details/amongcannibalsofoomcfa>.

Murray, J.H.P., *Papua or British New Guinea*, T. Fisher Unwin, 1912, <http://gutenberg.net.au/ebooks12/1202531h.html>.

Nalu, Malum, "The dawning of a new day for Ialibu." <http://malumnalu.blogspot.com.au/2011/09/dawning-of-new-day-for-ialibu.html>.

Nelson, Hank, Lutton, Nancy and Robertson, S. (eds), *Select Topics in the History of Papua and New Guinea*, University of Papua and New Guinea, Port Moresby, 1969.

Ninda, Yaluwin, "Miracles in Mt Hagen," *Niugini Nius,* 27 October 1989.

Niugini Nius, 26 April 1985.

Oates, Paul, "My Story: The making of a young patrol officer." <http://asopa.typepad.com/asopa_people/2013/03/my-story-the-making-of-a-young-patrol-officer.html#more>.

O'Neill, Peter, Concluding Address, Special Prayer Luncheon, State Function Room, National Parliament, 26 August 2014. <http://www.pm.gov.pg/images/SP-PM_Special_Prayer_Luncheon-140826F.pdf>.

Operation Tanim Bel, Life Outreach Team, Boroko, 1984.

Operation Tanim Bel: Arawa Crusade, Life Outreach Team, Boroko, 1985.

Operation Tanim Bel: Kimbe Crusade, Life Outreach Team, Boroko, 1986.

Operation Tanim Bel: Goroka Crusade, Life Outreach Team, Boroko, 1987.

Operation Tanim Bel: Lae Crusade, 1990; Wewak Crusade, 1991, Life Outreach Team, Boroko, 1991.

Peng, John, "Convert Criminals to Christianity," *Post-Courier*, 19 October 1984.

Senge, Frank, "Prime Minister agrees to meet gang leaders," *Post Courier*, July 1991.

Senge, Frank, "Criminals tell PM why they turn against people," *Post Courier*, 8 July 1991.

Sinclair, James, *The Explorations of Ivan Champion of Papua*, Pacific Press, Gold Coast, Australia, 1988.

Somare, Michael, *Sana*, Niugini Press, 1975.

Standish, Bill, "The Skate Era," *Papua New Guinea 1999: Crisis of Governance*, Parliament of Australia, Research Paper 4, 21 September 1999. <http://www.aph.gov.au/About_Parliament/Parliamentary_Departments/Parliamentary_Library/pubs/rp/rp9900/2000RP04#the>.

Strathern, Andrew. *Social Change in Pangia,* A paper presented to the Takuru Research Workshop, Pangia, 1985. Educational Research Unit, University of Papua New Guinea.

Trudgen, Richard, *Why Warriors Lie Down and Die,* Aboriginal Resource and Development Services Inc., Adelaide, 2000.

Uncle Graham and Grant Paulson, 'Forgive us our sins', 17 March 2015. <https://www.youtube.com/watch?v=YIUcZ_HBktU>.

Wallace, Alfred Russel, *The Malay Archipelago: The Land of the Orang-Utan, and the Bird of Paradise,* Vol. 2. Originally published 1869. Facsimile edition, Cambridge University Press, 2010.

Wallace, Alfred Russel, 'Narrative of Search after Birds of Paradise,' *Proceedings of the Zoological Society of London,* 1892.

BIBLIOGRAPHY

Weeks, Sheldon, *Education and Change in Pangia, Southern Highlands,* Educational Research Unit Report No. 56, April 1987.

Young, Michael W. and Clark, Julia, *An Anthropologist in Papua: The Photography of F.E. Williams, 1922–39,* Crawford House Publishing, Hindmarsh, SA, 2001.

Zurenuoc, Theodore, "Prayer and Repentance Day Speech," transcript in *Business Melanesia,* Issue 09, September 2014.

www.ingramcontent.com/pod-product-compliance
Lightning Source LLC
Chambersburg PA
CBHW072136160426
43197CB00012B/2126